Broadsheet Melbourne Food

A book by ● BROADSHEET

Contents

What to Eat & Where to Get It

Melbourne is one of the world's great food cities. There's a reason so many international chefs have put down roots here. We're a city that loves to dine out, and we have a vast pool of talented restaurateurs, chefs and waitstaff ready to inspire, excite and surprise us.

But that's only part of what makes Melbourne such an enviable eating and drinking destination. We're also surrounded by some of the most pristine oceans and farmland in the world. Gippsland is a hub for dairy and beef; Shepparton is the state's fruit bowl; and world-class oysters, crayfish and other seafood are pulled fresh from extensive tracts of Victoria's coastline.

In 2015, we published *The Broadsheet Melbourne Cookbook*, collecting recipes from the city's best chefs and restaurants. In this book, we're bringing you the city's finest ingredients. There's no reason a meal at home – whether in good company or by yourself – can't start with exactly the same produce used by the city's top chefs. But it's a big city. The range is vast, the scale intimidating.

The retailers and makers in this book have been chosen for their quality; the way they stand out from the crowd and dedicate themselves to their craft or cause. In these pages you'll find not only small producers (say, Damian the Mushroom Man at Prahran Market, whose three decades of service has seen him honoured with an Order of Australia), but larger businesses such as Ocean Made, which supplies restaurants such as Attica with the best ethically caught fish money can buy.

The book is broken down into easily digestible sections: grocers; delis; bakeries; butchers; fishmongers; sweets; bottle shops; cook & tableware; and coffee & tea. Four of Melbourne's best markets are included, with key stalls to visit. Advice and tips are scattered throughout. We see this book as a vital resource for the home cook and entertainer, as well as anyone who just likes eating good cheese. See you at the deli counter.

Shop with
the Seasons

We live in a time when nearly everything is available to buy year round. Tomatoes line supermarket shelves in June. Broccoli, kale and oranges fill them in the height of summer. There's no doubt it's convenient to nip to the shops to pick up whatever, whenever, but we don't need to tell you how good fruit and vegetables taste when harvested in their natural seasons. Better still when they haven't travelled far to get to you. This guide is plotted to tell you which produce is fine to pick up trans-seasonally, and which is best to hang out for until they're perfectly ripe (not to mention affordable). When in doubt, check your local farmers' market. Generally, they are spot-on barometers of freshness, seasonality and provenance.

YEAR ROUND

HERBS If you're not growing them yourself, it's easy to find fresh herbs in any season, although basil almost always tastes best in high summer. **RADISHES** Eat these soon after buying for maximum crunch, or refresh in iced water. **MUSHROOMS** Aside from special varieties such as pine mushrooms or morels, button and field mushrooms are easily grown, so accessible pretty much all year round. **ONIONS** Essential, and available, all year. **ALSO:** Avocados, carrots, lemons, lettuce, rocket, rhubarb, strawberries, spinach and yellow grapefruits.

SUMMER

BERRIES Blueberries, raspberries and blackberries are at their juiciest at the end of summer. **CHERRIES** No Christmas pavlova is complete without a tumble of shiny cherries at their peak. **BEANS** Eat these quickly to ensure they stay crunchy. When super fresh, they're fantastic raw and sliced. **MEDITERRANEAN VEGETABLES** Tomatoes, zucchinis, eggplants and capsicums are best as summer switches to autumn. **ALSO:** Apricots, currants, lychees, mangoes, mangosteens, nectarines, passionfruit, peaches, pomegranate, rockmelon, squash, sweetcorn, tomatoes, watermelon and zucchini.

AUTUMN

GRAPES Big, juicy, and at their peak in early autumn. Roast them on top of focaccia or ricotta for extra sweetness. **TURMERIC** Try fresh-grated turmeric and you'll never go back to the bright yellow powder again. **QUINCE** Slow roast and blend autumn's best quince to make a paste that will last you all year. **FIGS** The jewels of autumn are figs – look for sweet black and slightly firmer green varieties. **ALSO:** Apples, bok choy, Brussels sprouts, chestnuts, custard apples, eschallots, fennel, ginger, okra, pears, persimmons, pine mushrooms, plums, pomegranates and Swiss chard.

WINTER

BRASSICAS Leafy greens such as broccoli, cabbage and kale are best and most crisp after a few frosts. **PUMPKIN** Look out for many varieties of pumpkin in winter, from butternut and Jap to Queensland blue. **CELERIAC** Big, unwieldy celeriac bulbs are best slow-roasted or shredded raw with apple for a hearty winter salad. **MANDARINS** Don't even try to find tasty mandarins outside of winter, they simply don't exist **ALSO:** Beetroot, blood oranges, cauliflower, celery, cumquats, Jerusalem artichokes, kohlrabi, limes, oranges, parsnips, witlof and sweet potatoes.

SPRING

BROAD BEANS A bit of work to double-pod and blanch, but spring's first broad beans are worth the trouble. **MULBERRIES** Hunt for trees around your neighbourhood, or ask your grocer to order you a box of these glossy berries. **PAWPAW & PAPAYA** The perfect spring breakfast: fresh papaya with a squeeze of lime, eaten with a spoon. **ZUCCHINI FLOWERS** The start of the season brings zucchini flowers ready to stuff with cheese and deep-fry. **ALSO:** Asparagus, Asian greens, bananas, blueberries, chillies, cucumbers, globe artichokes, green beans, loquats, passionfruit, peas, pineapples, rockmelons, spring onions and watercress.

Bakeries

Keep the Air Out

Tivoli Road's baker Michael James stores his bread in an airtight bread box, and you should too. "Keeping the air out is the main thing. Once it oxidises, it goes stale quickly. Don't put it in the fridge. The cold air dries it out even more."

LUNE CROISSANTERIE

You have to be careful throwing around terms such as "world's best". That said, the croissants at Lune are, according to no lesser authority than the *New York Times*, the world's best. And they're right here, in Melbourne. Kate Reid is a qualified aerospace engineer and, as a *patissiere*, approaches each croissant with the precision she once applied to a Formula One car (she worked on the Williams team). Learning her (second) trade at legendary Paris boulangerie Du Pain et des Idées, Reid opened Lune's first incarnation in 2012. Word got around, and pre-dawn queues became the norm out front of her tiny Elwood shopfront. They're still common, even though Lune has relocated to a sizeable warehouse. In the centre of it, there's a futuristic glass-and-brick cube, kept at 18 degrees to ensure the notoriously temperature-sensitive pastries remain consistent. Another reason Lune's croissants are so exceptional is because it doesn't make many – around 8500 a week. Each is the result of a three-day process, and they're best experienced on the spot, straight from the oven. There are also excellent lemon-curd cruffins and pumpkin pies. Sign up for a mini-degustation at the Lune Lab; it's a three-course breakfast of experimental pastries with bottomless Small Batch coffee. **119 Rose Street, Fitzroy / 9419 2320 / Mo, Th & Fr 7.30am – 3pm, Sa & Su 8am – 3pm.**

ABOVE Lune Croissanterie.

LOAFER

Loafer's never had ambitions to conquer Melbourne. The bakery's MO has been the same since pastry chef Andrea Brabazon took over in 2007: the best ingredients, small batches and no shortcuts. On weekends, for example, there are just 250 baguettes for retail and wholesale customers to fight over. Loaves of wholemeal wheat, rye and spelt sourdough are in similarly short supply. The bakery has a reputation for its croissants, but don't miss the *kanelbullar* (cinnamon rolls) or *kardemummabullar* (cardamom rolls), both introduced by a visiting Swedish baker. **146 Scotchmer Street, Fitzroy North / 9489 0766 / Mo – Fr 7.30am – 5.30pm, Sa 7.30am – 3pm, Su 8am – 3pm.**

MILE END BAGELS

Mile End specialises in Montreal-style bagels, boiled in honey-water and baked in a wood-fired oven hand-built by Canadian stonemasons (really). That touch of smoke and fire sets these bagels apart. The outsides are crisp and the insides dense and vaguely sweet. The little rings get covered in classic sesame, poppy seeds, or cinnamon-raisin. Eat in and your bagel will come with peanut butter and jam, if you like, or the more exotic combination of edamame, smoked salmon, cucumber, Kewpie and black sesame oil. That said, cream cheese will do just fine, and is available here in several flavours. **14 – 16 Johnston Street, Fitzroy Mo – Su 7.30am – 3.30pm.**

You're probably already familiar with this perfectly formed bakery and its vanilla-bean custard bombolonis; faultlessly tart *pain aux raisin*; and collection of *viennoiseries* (sculptural croissants, glazed danishes with a shallow well of blueberry, pain au chocolat with a still-warm middle). It's difficult to list singular highlights without simply reeling off everything in the cabinet: the pistachio doughnut (and the tiramisu edition); the malty, rummy *canelés de Bordeaux*; the chocolate rye biscuits infused with Ecuadorian cacao. The sweets deserve every praise, but the savouries are no understudy. Daniel Chirico's whole-wheat sourdough is a bakery masterclass all its own; you'd expect nothing less from one of the country's most respected bakers. **149 Fitzroy Street, St Kilda / 9534 3777 / Tu – Th 7am – 4pm, Fr – Su 7am – 3pm. Other locations: Carlton, South Yarra.**

ALL ARE WELCOME

Once a Christian Science reading room, this Northcote bakery has embraced the site's liturgical roots by retaining the golden letters on the door as its name. A collaboration between baker Boris Portnoy – a former three-star Michelin pastry chef – and the Everyday Coffee team, the goodies here are determinedly global. Excellent (though somewhat expensive) sourdough sits alongside rare-for-Melbourne pastries such as seeded rye *ensaïmadas* (a sweet spiral pastry originating in Mallorca), *medovnik* (a Czech honey cake) and *khachapuri* (a traditional cheese-filled bread from the Republic of Georgia). Make sure you try Portnoy's take on pain au chocolat, the sweet and swirly Gianduja Babka Bun. **190 High Street, Northcote / Mo – Sa 7am – 4pm, Su 8am – 4pm.**

TIVOLI ROAD BAKERY

Michael James's commitment to his loaves is inspiring. The Cornish baker rises at 3am each day to light his ovens and knead. Each bun gets wrapped in a couche cloth (like canvas) and proved over two days, coaxing caramel tones from organic flour, which later sets like magma into a blistered crust. Besides the headline sourdough, Tivoli Road makes a range of subtle variations: soy and linseed; rye; spelt; fruit; multigrain; and olive. As special as these loaves are, it's okay to admit you're here for the doughnuts, particularly the show-stopping lemon custard. But don't overlook the other sweets: Tivoli Road's pastries are a highlight of any occasion that includes them. **3 Tivoli Road, South Yarra / 9041 4345 / Mo – Su 7.30am – 4pm.**

LEFT Baker D. Chirico. **ABOVE** Tivoli Road Bakery.

AGATHÉ PATISSERIE

Agathé Kerr is no traditionalist. She's trained at the great pastry institutions – L'École de Boulangerie et de Pâtisserie in Paris and Pâtisserie Lenôtre – but her creations are a little more idiosyncratic. A croissant might be glazed in Earl Grey, then infused with pandan or laksa. Purists will be pacified by her Cannelé Bordeaux, baked so caramel they're almost black, or by the attenuated layers of puff pastry blanketed in apple. **322–326 Coventry Street, South Melbourne / We, Fr–Su 8am–4pm.**

A1 LEBANESE BAKERY

Since opening in 1992, A1 has set the standard for wholemeal Lebanese-style pita bread in this city. There's an endless stream of pizza and pie flowing from the ovens at this Brunswick institution, from thinly stretched za'atar-covered numbers, to fat little pies with lemon-dressed spinach and Danish feta. Stock up on pomegranate molasses and jars of pickles, and take a honey-drunk baklava for the road. **643–645 Sydney Road, Brunswick / 9386 0440 / Mo–We 7am–7pm, Th–Sa 7am–9pm.**

BAKER BLEU

As a kid Mike Russell was known as "Blue", thanks to his strawberry-blond hair. He's revived the nickname here – in French. Russell has worked at Sydney's Bourke Street Bakery and Iggy's Down Under, and Baker D. Chirico here. At Bleu, he works exclusively with sourdough. Bagels, baguettes, white and rye loaves are fermented for 18 hours, resulting in beautiful, caramel-coloured crusts favoured by many of Melbourne's top restaurants. Rotating specials feature ancient grains such as spelt, purple wheat and kamut. **260 Glen Eira Road, Elsternwick / Th–Su 7.30am–sold out.**

WOODFROG BAKERY

Lithobates sylvaticus is a hardy frog that can survive more than half its body freezing solid. It's the mascot for Jarrod Hack's bakery and embodies his adaptive philosophy. Case in point: the baguette, made with regular baker's yeast, rather than the usual sourdough. It proves for 25 hours, developing a deep, instantly recognisable smell. Woodfrog can be found all over town, but everything is baked in St Kilda's stone ovens. **108 Barkly Street, St Kilda / 9077 5440 / Mo–Su 7am–5pm. Other locations: Brighton, Camberwell, Doncaster, Kew, CBD, Southbank.**

CANDIED BAKERY

Back in 2012, chef Toula Ploumidis and baker Orlando Artavilla took a trip to the United States. Now they make a huge range of sweets and savouries that reference Australia and America alike. Their take on the Drake's Coffee Cake (for *Seinfeld* fans) features a vanilla-butter crumb and cinnamon streusel. Sweet pies rotate between flavours such as Oreo, apple and key lime. Then there are apple pie shakes, matcha white chocolate soft serve and flaky beef pies. **Hudsons Road, Spotswood / 9391 1335 / Tu–Sa 7am–4pm, Su 8am–4pm.**

FATTO A MANO

Sandwiches get the respect they're due at Fatto a Mano, where small loaves are designed especially to carry ripe tomato and wedges of brie. With all-organic ingredients and a decade-old sourdough starter, Mario and Sandra Cucuzza bake classic high-tin and light-rye loaves, as well as cornbread and spelt versions. Their plump spinach and ricotta cheese triangles are dusted with sesame and crimped down with a fork. Thai chicken sausage rolls make a compelling argument for fusion. **228 Gertrude Street, Fitzroy / 9417 5998 Tu–Sa 6am–6pm.**

RIGHT Baker D. Chirico.

Breakfast at Home

with JEAN THAMTHANAKORN
& SARIN ROJANAMETIN

When Sunday rolls around, plenty of chefs will do anything to avoid the kitchen. Nora's Jean Thamthanakorn and Sarin Rojanametin can't wait to get back in. "I love to cook," Rojanametin says. "I don't really eat out. I just love cooking at home because: one, I get to cook different stuff and two, it's just nice. It's relaxing for me."

A BROADSHEET BOOK

The couple lives within walking distance of Meatsmith (pg.88) in Fitzroy, which is their first stop for ingredients. Besides charcuterie – which they like to put on toast – Meatsmith is an excellent source of specialty sauces, oils and dry goods.

After Meatsmith, they walk down the block to The Source Bulk Foods to get ingredients for granola: nuts, blueberries, goji berries, quinoa and amaranth. "I like the fact there's very little packaging at Source," Rojanametin says. Adding spices such as clove, cinnamon, nutmeg to your granola mix always makes it more unique and delicious.

Thamthanakorn is a bread-maker who doesn't just bake, but mills fresh grains for flour, too. "We heat our bread in a dry pan on medium heat, which makes the crumb very light, crunchy and airy," Rojanametin says.

Sundays are a rare time for Rojanametin and Thamthanakorn to sit down and enjoy what they do for other people all week. "We don't have time to eat. The only two days we get to eat at home are our two days off," Rojanametin says. "The main goal, really, is just to buy healthy stuff and eat healthy stuff."

Grocers

Nunziata and Pasqual Toscano began selling fresh fruit and veg in 1950, and their grandkids are still doing it today. Unlike modern supermarkets, Toscano's puts the spotlight on ingredients when they're in season. In autumn there are Russet Burbank spuds from Boneo and fresh chestnuts from Bright. In winter, it's all about Cara Cary Ruby oranges, truffles from Mole Creek in Tasmania and pomegranates and early-season asparagus direct from Mildura. In spring there are zucchini flowers and gooseberries, and in late summer a crop of Shepard avocados and Carolina Reaper chillies (until recently, the hottest variety in the world). For cooks in the market for more unusual ingredients, Toscano's is one of the few grocers stocking fresh native ingredients such as samphire, saltbush and lemon myrtle. Alongside the fresh produce is a diverse range of continental essentials: pasta, vinegars and confectionary imported by Casa Italia; bread by Baker D. Chirico (pg.26); top-quality small goods from both Italy and Australia; and giant wheels of parmesan that Pat Toscano shaves by hand. **215–219 High Street, Kew / 9853 7762 Mo–Th 8am–6pm, Fr 8am–7pm, Sa 7.30am–5pm. Other locations: Richmond, Hawksburn.**

Say No to Cold Eggs

If you're eating them within a week, eggs don't need be kept in the fridge. You'll also get the best results from your baking when you use room-temperature eggs.

TERRA MADRE

To many people, Terra Madre is synonymous with organic and wholefoods shopping in Melbourne. Every weekend the aisles are stuffed with people squeezing past one another to get to the fair-trade adzuki beans and phosphate-free facial scrubs. Often you'll find a pyramid constructed entirely of Bonsoy or Sunny Queen Eggs, and there's a startling array of conscientious brands such as Loving Earth; Belmore Meats; Pana Chocolate (pg.106); Zeally Bay Sourdough; and Peace, Love and Vegetables. Fresh Demeter-certified pomegranates come straight from farmers in Echuca, feijoas are from Gippsland, and you'll find wild-foraged pine mushrooms when they're in season. There's an exhaustive selection of organic pulses, grains, flours, dried fruits and nuts that Terra Madre packages itself. Cleaning products are devoid of ugly chemicals, whether for the bathroom or kitchen. On the street front you'll find freshly cut bouquets of native flowers. Upstairs, Terra Madre runs a clinic with qualified naturopaths, acupuncturists, massage therapists and kinesiologists who can guide patients through the store's range of vitamins, supplements and herbal mixes. Just be prepared to use your elbows. **103 High Street, Northcote / 9489 5824 / Mo – Su 8.30am – 7.30pm.**

CLAY HEALTH & ORGANICS

Inside this former terrace house you'll find the finer things: Holy Goat chèvre and Pepe Saya Butter; sourdough from Loafer (pg.25) and Baker D. Chirico (pg.26); fresh boxes of tortillas from La Tortilleria; and biodynamic wine from Pennyweight in Beechworth. All the fruits and vegetables are hand-harvested by a fifth-generation farmer, and cold-pressed juices are made on-site. The knowledgeable staff has backgrounds in organics, naturopathy, nutrition and environmental science. When there's time, they'll even carry your groceries to your car or nearby home. **719–721 Rathdowne Street, Carlton North / 9349 3957 Mo–Fr 9am–7pm, Sa & Su 9am–6pm.**

SMITH & MALONEY

This neat little store on the upper reaches of Lygon Street is the quintessential local grocer. With a street-facing bar for freshly squeezed juice or a coffee, hanging about for a chat is actively encouraged. There's a trim selection of seasonal fruit and veg that tends toward the organic, and an assortment of good-for-you products including Earnest Bean tofu, Naked Locals soup, Dalhousie Organic jams, Bite Me falafels and Meadows Free Range slow-roasted chook, as well as vegan-friendly wines by Tamburlaine and Freehand. **157 Lygon Street, Brunswick East / 9381 1416 / Mo – Fr 8.30am – 6.30pm, Sa & Su 8.30am – 5.30pm.**

HINOKI JAPANESE PANTRY

Hayato Takasaka couldn't use *hinoki* (timber from Japanese cypress) to fit out his store, but it has a clean, natural look thanks to the closest available alternative – beech. The minimalist scheme puts the focus on what you'll find on the shelves: Pocky sticks, green-tea Kit Kats, mammoth Kewpie mayonnaise bottles and other colourfully packaged treats. There's also gyoza, curries, ramen, *koroke* (croquettes), udon noodles and a respectable range of Japanese alcohols. The in-house sushi counter, where everything is sliced to order, is excellent. **279 Smith Street, Fitzroy / 9417 4531 / Tu – Th 10am – 6pm, Fr & Sa 10am – 7pm, Su 11am – 5pm.**

KT MART ASIAN GROCERY

Korean expats feel right at home in this two-storey minimart, which stocks everything from bulgogi marinades and mulberry tea, to skin lotion and *onggi* earthenware for fermenting kimchi. There's a small selection of Japanese, Thai and Vietnamese products, but the main event is dozens of varieties of pre-made kimchi and frozen Korean barbeque meats such as *samgyeopsal* (pork belly) and *galbisal* (rib meat). Fresh fruit and veg is about the only thing missing, because the Queen Victoria Market (pg.72) is walking distance. **600 Elizabeth Street, Melbourne / 0478 801 827 / Mo – Su 10am – 11pm 515 Whitehorse Road, Mitcham / 0421 992 779 Mo – Su 9am – 9pm.**

RIPE THE ORGANIC GROCER

All fruit and veg at Ripe is certified organic and Australian grown, without exception. You might find Creole garlic from Tasmania, freshly picked watercress or a disorienting number of obscure apple varieties, such as Belle de Broksopp, Mutsu and Cox orange pippin (like we said, disorienting). For those on specific diets there's gluten-free sourdough and cold-pressed coconut oil; ethically sourced bone broths; natural skin and haircare; and an enormous range of grains and pulses. **Shop 7, Prahran Market, 163 Commercial Road, Prahran / 9804 8606 / Tu, Th – Sa 6am – 5pm, Su 9am – 3pm.**

WILD THINGS

Every grocer should have an ugly bin. The fruit and veg at Wild Things may not be uniformly shaped or waxed to a high sheen, but that's beside the point. Like all the produce, they're reliably delicious and reliably ethically sourced. All meat is hormone and nitrate free; all eggs are free range; and all packaging compostable. Paleo, vegan and vego diets are welcomed with open arms. Skincare, vitamins and cleaning products are naturally derived. And there's ice-cream. **228 – 230 Street Georges Road, Fitzroy North / 9939 6670 Mo – Fr 9am – 7.30pm, Sa 8.30am – 7pm, Su 9.30am – 7pm.**

LEO'S FINE FOOD & WINE

Not many supermarkets play Spanish flamenco and Italian opera non-stop. But then, not many are stocked like Leo's. It makes fresh orange juice every day; sells coffee beans by weight; and packages fine Australian and European cheeses at a dedicated counter. There are also extensive sections for Italian, Mexican, Indian, Japanese, Chinese, Thai, Jewish and Middle Eastern food. But it's not elitist – if you need Smith chips, Omo laundry powder or Weet-Bix, it has them, too. **26 Princess Street, Kew / 9243 3777 / Mo – Su 7am – 10pm. Other locations: Heidelberg, Hartwell.**

LEFT Clay Health & Organics.

PLUMP ORGANIC

Jock Campbell and Emma Byrnes opened Plump Organic in Yarraville largely because it was close to Melbourne Market, on Footscray Road. That was in 2002. Since 2015 the market has been in Epping, an hour's drive away. Campbell is still there at 4am each morning to secure the best in-season Australian organic produce for his customers, such as biodynamic stone fruits grown near Ruffy, Footscray cucumbers and Slaty Creek garlic. All that's piled high along one side of the store. The other side is reserved for condiments, honey and herbs, as well as hand-blended teas and environmentally friendly laundry powder, shampoo, conditioner and make-up. In the fridges you'll find reliably delicious Milawa chickens, frozen berries and dairy-free ice-creams. **24 Ballarat Street, Yarraville / 9687 6422 / Mo – Fr 9am – 6.30pm, Sa 9am – 4pm.**

POMPELLO

Where many supermarkets stock two kinds of spuds (washed and dirty), Pompello has 10: midnight pearls darker than a beetroot, waxy kipflers meant for the saucepan, fluffy Dutch creams and Russian blues. Founded by Mark Cafarella, Pompello arrived in Seddon long before gentrification. It's now managed by son Elliott, who shifted the focus to local and organic. Passionfruits, when in season, come in baseball-sized Panama varieties and the more golf ball-esque misty gem. Later in summer, there's a cult following for "Doncaster tomatoes" from a seasoned Italian grower in East Mitcham. All year round there's little tinted bowtie pasta, and the Grampians' finest olive oil from Mount Zero. Elliot stocks fresh flowers every day, which he chooses by deciding which look the most cheerful. **164 Victoria Street, Seddon / 9687 2627 / Mo – Sa 8am – 6.30pm.**

AUNT MAGGIE'S

At Aunt Maggie's, "organic food" is simply referred to as "food". What passes for edible is defined as much by what it doesn't include (pesticides, chemicals), as what it does. You'll find certified organic, in-season fruit and vegetables including purple cauliflower; fresh gluten-free pasta and gnocchi by Ardor Food Co.; the entire range of Global Organics canned beans; Ethical Foods coconut oil; and Richie's fresh salsas. There's organic beer and wine; raw and gluten-free cereals; and a range of natural shampoos, conditioners, moisturisers and cleaning products. The grocer is inspired by the memory of one woman: co-owner Wayne Ferrell's aunt Maggie, a skilled cook who worked exclusively with chemical-free fruit, vegetables and chickens in the 1960s. **188 Gertrude Street, Fitzroy / 9417 5504 / Mo–Fr 8.30am–7pm, Sa 9am–6pm, Su 10am–6pm. Other locations: Malvern, Carlton.**

THE COMMON GOOD

After escaping the corporate world, Meneka Premkumar and John Currey went in search of a better life in 2013 and found it in The Common Good. Built entirely from recycled, reclaimed and foraged materials, this Hawthorn grocer is adamant everything it sells be ethically produced. You'll find lovably ugly fruit and vegetables sourced directly from farmers, much organically grown, even if not certifiably so. Staples are all excellent quality: bread is delivered daily from neighbourhood baker Knead; Jonesy's provides the milk; eggs are from Golden Yolk; and meat's from Berties Butcher (pg.89) in Richmond. There are also plenty of skin and healthcare products from manufacturers such as Jacqueline Evans and Red Seal. **77 Church Street, Hawthorn 9077 3431 / Mo–Fr 8.30am–6.30pm, Sa 8.30am –5pm.**

MINH PHAT

Cooking Vietnamese, Thai, Korean, Chinese, Japanese or Malay? Get to Minh Phat. You'll find everything you need at this no-frills supermarket: fresh noodles and bao; Shaoxing wine, Doubanjiang paste and Chinkiang vinegar; dried wood-ear mushrooms, lotus seeds and Sichuan peppercorns; bulk-size bottles of peanut oil, fish-sauce and soy; and all the Sriracha you'll ever want for. There's also a select range of fresh produce such as salted duck eggs, bean-shoots and winter melon, along with frozen abalone and squid. You can even buy the gear you need to cook with, from bamboo steamers to razor-sharp knives. It's no wonder the place is indispensable to the local Vietnamese community and many further afield. 2–8 Nicholson Street, Abbotsford / 9429 4028 / Mo – Su 9am – 7pm.

THE LEAF STORE

Leon Mugavin has been a grocer for 30 years. Once a market stall holder, Mugavin now channels his enthusiasm for organic produce into Leaf, his Ormond Village grocer. There's a considerable range of fresh fruit and vegetables brought in daily, as well as goods from producers such as Padre Coffee, Red Hill Muesli, Willunga Pasta, Irrewarra Sourdough and ethical meat producer Cherry Tree Organics. More than 800 products (including milk) are available online for same-day delivery, too. 111–113 Ormond Road, Elwood / 9531 6542 Mo – Th 6am – 8pm, Fr – Su 7am – 7pm. 112 Were Street, Brighton / 9592 1928 / Mo – Su 7am – 7pm.

GEWÜRZHAUS

If your cookbook demands you add a teaspoon of ajowan, a pinch of annatto seeds, or a sprinkling of Persian blue salt, visit Gewürzhaus ("geh-voortz-hows"), where 350 dried spices, herbs, salts, teas and sugars are stocked by the tub. It's not really a grocer as such, but when it comes to cooking, it's too useful to pass over. Past unblended spices such as ground chipotle chillies, native pepperberry and classic oregano, there are 100-plus pre-mixed blends, including African berbere, Viennese christmas sugar and Aussie meat pie. Cooking classes are run in-house, so you can learn how to use it all, too. 342 Lygon Street, Carlton / 9348 4815 / Mo – Sa 10am – 6pm, Su 11am – 5pm. Other locations: Hawksburn, CBD, Chadstone, Queen Victoria Market.

SUZURAN GROCERY

Since 1979, this Camberwell grocer has been selling superior matcha and *genmaicha* (rice green tea); buckwheat noodles and bonito flakes; and, of course, Koshihikari, the King of Rice. There's a selection of choice sake and Japanese beer, as well as specialty Osechi foods for the festival season, such as *datemaki* (sweet omelette mixed with fish cake) and *kuri kinton* (mashed sweet potato and chestnuts). Sushi-grade fish is brought in daily, which you can eat in-store, or take home and prepare yourself. 1025–1027 Burke Road, Camberwell / 9882 2349 / Tu – Th 9am – 6pm, Fr 9am – 8pm, Sa 9am – 7pm, Su 10am – 3.30pm.

Hardy herbs such as rosemary and thyme can be wrapped in a damp paper towel and kept in an airtight plastic bag in the fridge.

Bigger-leaved herbs such as basil, parsley and coriander can be kept in water in a jar on the kitchen bench.

Pantry Favourites

with PITZY FOLK

Capi founder Pitzy Folk doesn't just talk about "the good life" – he lives it. At his South Melbourne home, the man behind the mineral water grows mandarins, figs, almonds, basil, sage, peaches, chillies, citrus, avocados, cherries, nectarines, quinces, blueberries, raspberries and bananas with great success. He and wife Anne have been involved in Melbourne's eating and drinking scene for more than 40 years across several businesses, including the Observatory Cafe in the Royal Botanic Gardens.

"We go to the markets, we grow our own vegetables, I'm a fisherman, I love my fresh fish and all this," Folk says, waving a hand at his garden. "I eat too much and I drink too much, but that's what good life is about." Unfortunately, he can't grow everything he needs. Here are a few other essential ingredients for Pitzy Folk's good life.

FRESH HERBS FROM HIS GARDEN

"I don't use any dried herbs. The only thing I sometimes use is Greek oregano, which I buy in bundles at the market. I grow rosemary, parsley, oregano, thyme, dill, tarragon and chives at home. It makes a huge difference."

MURRAY RIVER SEA SALT

"You couldn't possibly get anything better. It's a small business and it works to reduce salinity in the Murray-Darling Basin. It tastes good and the flakes are great."

SHERRY VINEGAR

"Sherry vinegar's a big thing for me. A 25-year-old one from Spain is the perfect dressing for salads."

EGGS

"I hate battery eggs. I buy my eggs from Field, Barns & Co at the South Melbourne Market. They taste like eggs should taste."

CHICKEN STOCK

"I don't like stock cubes, I prefer to make my own with organic quality chicken. It's really easy. If you want to save money, buy a carcass at any market, put it in a pot with celery, carrots, onion, peppercorns and parsley, then boil it for a few hours. You can freeze it afterwards and use it as you need."

BUTTER

"I also love the butter at Field, Barns & Co, which is 100 per cent natural, with no preservatives and made on the premises. It tastes like butter used to taste, when you grew up as a kid."

PAPRIKA

"I love Spanish food. There's always paprika in my pantry, smoked or plain varieties. It's great for chicken, and in any marinades for the grill."

WASABI

"I'm addicted to wasabi. I have it in ham sandwiches and on steak instead of horseradish or English mustard. I grow the plants and use the leaves in salads, but Melbourne's climate is too warm to produce good roots. Sometimes I find the Tasmanian roots at South Melbourne (pg.70) or Prahran Market (pg.69), otherwise I just buy the cheapest Japanese brand in a tube."

ORTIZ ANCHOVIES

"Are there any other anchovies? They're the best there are."

Delicatessens

Holy Goat Organic
Brigid's Well
$13.50
per 100g

Holy Goat Organic
La Luna Ring
$13.50 per
Sutton Grange,
Victor   100g

Colston Bassett
Stilton
Nottinghamshire, ENG
Neal's Yard Dairy
$12.50 per 100g

Berry's
P
Gippsl
Buffalo Milk

Delice de Bourgogne
Burgundy, FRA
Triple Cream Brie
$8²⁰ per 100g

Jean Grogne
ile de France, FR
Triple Cream Bri
$9.

per 100g
t Blue
e.

St. Vernier
washed in Savagnin
Jura, France
$15 ea

Carles Roquefort
Raw Sheep's milk.
France.
$14 per 100g

MEDITERRANEAN WHOLESALERS

Mediterranean Wholesalers was started by Giuseppe and Carmela Madafferi in 1961 and is now one of Australia's largest continental food stores. It's strange to think it started as a plain old milk bar. Its long linoleum-floored aisles are home to more than 250 varieties of pasta, from fresh tubes of penne, to little candy-coloured bowties, ear-shaped orecchiette and twirled ribbons of fusilli al ferretto. Whole aisles are devoted to jars of antipasti; Borelli Mare pickled octopus is nestled up against Carmellina pickled mushrooms. At the deli counter you'll find San Daniele prosciutto; capocollo and bresaola; bocconcini; provolone; and aged Parmigiano-Reggiano. There's even a dedicated Italian liquor section (meloncello, anyone?) and a cookware section where you can pick up hand-crank cheese graters and pots large enough to conceal a small child. **482 Sydney Road, Brunswick / 9380 4777 / Mo–Th 9am–5.30pm, Fr 9am–6pm, Sa 8.30am–2pm.**

BILL'S FARM

School excursions are generally run for the benefit of students, but in the case of former secondary-school maths teacher Bill Tzimas, the gain was all his. On one school trip he re-discovered the joys of market shopping and chose to dedicate himself to cheese there and then. That was nearly 30 years ago. Now he's a qualified cheese grader, a judge for the Australian Grand Dairy Awards and one of the best cheesemongers in town. Under the glass you'll find haloes of Holy Goat's La Luna, fromage de Meaux direct from the Brie region, and freshly moulded mozzarella by Vannella cheese in Cairns. To accompany all that dairy, Tzimas also stocks silvery Italian anchovies, genuine foie gras, barrel-aged vinegars and all the hits in cured meat: mettwurst, casalinga and saucisson. **Shop 17–20, Dairy Hall, Queen Victoria Market, 20/155 Victoria Street, Melbourne / 9328 2003 / Tu, Th 6am–2pm, Fr 6am–4.30pm, Sa 6am–3pm, Su 8.30am–3.30pm.**

ABOVE Mediterranean Wholesalers.

D.O.C. is the deli Melbourne's original Italian suburb deserves. It might be small, but it packs in a huge range of products, many of them hard to find elsewhere. On the cheese front, there's pecorino, Parmigiano-Reggiano and springy white balls of mozzarella floating in a bath of buffalo milk. More novel items imported direct from Italy include Gia Cometta *crema gia duja* (hazelnut chocolate cream); *gelatina birra* (a craft-beer jelly that goes with cheese, steak or even cakes) and Il Trullo preserved porcini mushrooms from Puglia. There are 100-year-old balsamic vinegars and a range of olive oils that acknowledge the strength of our local product alongside those from Italia. The team at D.O.C. knows not everything is better when it's made in Italy – the fresh pasta rolled out by its chefs being the most notable example. **330 Lygon Street, Carlton / 9347 8482 / Mo – Sa 9am – 7pm, Su 10am – 7am.**

Don't Suffocate Your Cheese

Cheesemonger Olivia Sutton of Harper & Blohm (pg.63) has a pro-tip for keeping fromage: "As soon as you get home, remove any cling-film and wrap your cheese in baking paper. Then put it in a container with a damp Chux over the bottom to stop your cheese drying out."

A BROADSHEET BOOK

TWO TALL CHEFS

Carlton's not short on cheese, but Two Tall Chefs remains indispensable to locals. Founded by former Michelin-star chef Monte Hudson, who's logged time with Philippe Mouchel, Tetsuya Wakuda and Armando Percuoco, the deli and cafe is home to a number of hard-to-find cheeses. We're into Perl Las from Caws Cenarth in Wales, an organic cow's-milk number made on 100-year-old cast-iron presses; and 13th-generation cheesemaker Ian Fowler's clothbound cheddar, matured for 12 months on pine boards. Closer to home, there's the King River Gold, a washed-rind cheese made by the store's former tenants, Milawa Cheese. No one cheese stays in the cabinet long and customers are encouraged to make requests. **665 Nicholson Street, Carlton North / 9381 1777 / Tu & We 9am–5pm, Th–Sa 9am–10pm, Su 9am–5.30pm.**

MILK THE COW

Why it took so long for Melbourne to get its first licensed cheese bar is anyone's guess. Milk the Cow stocks more than 180 varieties in its pungent open cabinet including oozing cow's milk Le Duc Vacherin from Franche-Comté, France; Quickes mature cheddar from Devon in the UK; and Woodside Cheesewrights' The Kid, a raw-milk goat cheese produced in South Australia. Everything can be taken home, but we absolutely recommend sticking around for a matched wine, cider, sake, whisky or beer tasting flight. The last two particularly – yeasty and malty flavours often pair well with cheese. **1/157 Fitzroy Street, St Kilda / 9537 2225 / Mo–Th 12pm–11pm, Fr & Sa 12pm–1am, Su 12pm–11pm. 323 Lygon Street, Carlton / 9348 4771 / Su–Th 12pm–late, Fr & Sa 12pm–1am.**

STOCKED FOOD STORE

If you want to give your larder the effortless abundance of a country kitchen without the trouble of actually cooking, Stocked Food Store's the place for you. Head to the deli counter to carve off a few slices of house-roasted beef, pack up a couple of chargrilled chicken fillets and a tub full of chilli-marinated mussels. There are thick wedges of sopressa and vacuum-sealed spicy cacciatore, as well as pre-cooked salmon patties, summer salads, and meatballs in red sauce. On the flipside, all the basic ingredients are here for you to cook yourself: pasta both fresh and dried, bags of black rice, handmade stocks and DIY sushi kits. **549 Malvern Road, Toorak / 9826 3333 / Mo–Fr 7am–6pm, Sa 7am–5pm. 130 Glenferrie Road / 9576 1910 Mo–Fr 7am–6pm, Sa 7am–5pm.**

SMITH STREET ALIMENTARI

Whether or not you can cook, Alimentari's ready -made meals are a compelling reason to leave your oven cold and your pans clean. Pork-and-fennel lasagne is a mid-week favourite, the rotisserie chicken's always banging, and the kitchen takes all the work out of sugo and stock. Along the right wall, there are bags of Veneziano coffee, huge jars of McClure's pickles from Detroit and a decent range of salts and olive oils. When you're entertaining, turn to the selection of cold-cuts: cured salumi, capocollo, bresaola and 'nduja by Victorian producers, or pork rillettes, chicken-liver pate and terrines made in-house. For a well-rounded grazing platter, add some parmesan and a bowl of marinated champignons. **302 Smith Street, Collingwood / 9416 1666 / Mo–Su 8am–6pm.**

LEFT Smith Street Alimentari.

CASA IBERICA

Without Casa Iberica, would there be restaurants Movida, Nomada or Bomba? For more than 40 years, the graffiti-covered corner has been Melbourne's ark of Hispanic culture. The store opened in 1973 when founders Alice and Jose de Sousa migrated from the tiny Portuguese island of Madeira, and in recent years was taken on by their godson, Paulo. The name refers to the entire Iberian Peninsula: Spain and Portugal, and also – spiritually and culinarily at least – Central and South America. In a relatively tiny space you'll find an astonishing array of ingredients: jars of dulce de leche caramel spread; chimichurri salsa; hard-to-find yucca; heart of palm; and patacones, little pieces of green plantain. But wait, there's more: calimenta marmalade and real-deal piri piri direct from Portugal; Argentinian yerba mate tea; sour Brazilian manioc starch; and Peruvian purple corn pudding. While the list of esoteric ingredients is definitely impressive, all the basic elements are here in abundance: tick off ancho, mulato, habanero, chipotle and poblano chillies; raid the upright fridge stacked with fresh tortillas; carve off a wafer of the finest jamón; and take home tins of Los Novios paprika in both the smoked and sweet iterations. You can even buy a paella pan to cook it all in. **25 Johnston Street, Fitzroy / 9419 4420 Mo – Th 7.30am – 6pm, Fr 7.30am – 7pm, Sa 7.30am – 2pm. 154 – 156 Fulham Road, Alphington 9497 2107 / Tu – Sa 9.30am – 3pm.**

ABOVE Casa Iberica. **RIGHT** Spring Street Grocer.

SPRING STREET GROCER

From the street, this looks like a gelataria. Which it is, partly. Squeeze past the cone-toting crowd to stuff your basket with some of Europe and Australia's finest smallgoods, including golden tins of Pollastrini sardines; blood-red bottles of Pastificio Venturino passata; squat little jars of Tuscan porcini mushrooms; bulk-size boxes of Mount Zero olive oil from the Grampian Ranges, and McClure's benchmark-setting pickles from Detroit. Then, follow your nose down the adjacent orange spiral staircase to the cheese-stuffed basement for a wheel of Comté, or a wedge of Tasmania's premiere raw-milk cheese, the Bruny Island C2. It's an impressive collection – we'd expect nothing less from Con Christopoulos, the discerning restaurateur behind Butcher's Diner, The European, Emilia and The French Saloon. **157 Spring Street, Melbourne / 9639 0335 Mo–Th 8am–9pm, Fr 8am–10pm, Su 9am–9pm.**

MAKER & MONGER

Anthony Femia is a literal scholar among cheese-mongers. He was awarded a Jack Green Churchill Fellowship to study affinage, the practice of ageing and maturing cheese. He started at London's Neal's Yard Dairy before moving to France to work alongside internationally lauded cheese-makers Herve Mons and Rodolphe Le Meunier. At Maker & Monger he trades in incredibly select cheeses: Carles roquefort made from raw sheep's milk and Brillat Savarin triple-cream brie; Rogue Creamery's heady American Caveman Blue, and local strokes of genius by Holy Goat. You can learn an incredible amount chatting with the staff, and you should absolutely do it over one of its moreish grilled-cheese sandwiches, or raclette dripping over potatoes, mushrooms and pickles. Or both. **Prahran Market, 163–181 Commercial Road, South Yarra, Stall 25 / Tu, Th & Fr 8am–4pm, Sa 7.30am–4.30pm, Su 9.30am–3pm.**

A BROADSHEET BOOK

THAT'S AMORE

Giorgio Linguanti was raised in the Sicilian town of Syracuse and picked up a job in a cheese factory when he arrived in Australia. It was there that he discovered his great love: bocconcini. At his Thomastown outlet, the little globules of deliciousness are available fresh, hand-pulled and hand-moulded using the morning's milk. Linguanti has continued to expand his offering to include a whole range of Italian dairy, including salted ricotta, smoked caciocavallo, burrata, diavoletti, fior di latte and his signature buffalo mozzarella, which you absolutely mustn't miss. That's Amore also has a sideline in other Sicilian staples: porchetta, pannetone and pasta. **66 Latitude Boulevard, Thomastown / 9463 4200 / Mo–Su 8am–5pm.**

PSARAKOS

Hard to pronounce, but easy to love. This family-run Greek grocer has been doing its thing since 1972, starting with fresh fruit and veg. In time, it's expanded to carry European specialties at its in-house deli, nut shop and liquor store. It's worth coming here for traditional Greek pastries such as bougasta and spanikopita; freshly scooped tubs of jet-black olives; kinked sausages with dusty white rinds; and Olympian Bakery's Sweet Loaf. Tuck a bottle of retsina into your basket, too – everything's improved by pine-flavoured wine. **2/8 Clarendon Street, Thornbury / 9484 1991 Mo–Fr 9am–6pm, Sa 8am–4pm.**

BOCCACCIO CELLARS

Boccaccio is unique among IGA-branded supermarkets. Run by the D'Anna family for well over 50 years, this Mediterranean heaven was modelled on the groundbreaking department stores Le Bon Marche in Paris and Eataly in Milan. It houses more than 3000 wines the D'Annas import personally, and there's an entire wall stocked with prosciutto flown in from Parma. We recommend a chat with in-house cheesemongers Bernard and Jerry, who'll help you select from the best in Euro dairy as well as 500 local varieties. **1030–1050 Burke Road, Balwyn / 1300 262 222 / Mo–Su 7am–7pm.**

SMITH & DELI

If vegan is no longer a dirty word, then in Melbourne that's partly thanks to Shannon Martinez and Mo Wyse. As at round-the-corner restaurant Smith & Daughters, at Smith & Deli, omnivores genuinely won't even notice their pastrami on rye isn't really made with meat. Same goes for the take-home lasagne, the milk-free mozzarella and the homemade vegan aioli, which is velvety with an umami punch. It also stocks products such as Daiya cheese, Tofurky sausages, vegan lollies, and "meats" by Field Roast. Taking five days to make, Martinez's croissant is a butterless wonder: flaky crescents hiding silken inner layers, the Holy Grail of vegan baking. **111 Moor Street, Fitzroy / 9042 4117 / Tu–Sa 8am–6pm.**

HARPER & BLOHM

Growing up on King Island is a pretty handy start for anyone entering the cheese industry. Still, Olivia Sutton has put the hard yards into her profession, spending 10 years at Calendar Cheese Company and working in Dublin's exemplary Sheridans Cheesemongers. Visit her little Essendon boutique for mouldy wonders such as Red Hill blue, fleur de Maquis, Epoisses, Prom Country white mould, Bruny Island's raw-milk creations, L'Artisan's washed-rind Mountain Man and special editions of Holy Goat. **80 Primrose Street, Essendon We & Th 12.30pm–6pm, Fr & Sa 10am–6pm, Su 12pm–4pm.**

KAZACHOK EASTERN EUROPEAN DELI

Kazachok: a Russian folk dance that involves lots of squats and high kicks. Also Kazachok: a Russian deli that involves lots of house-made smallgoods. Pork is king here, appearing in salamis, kabanas and traditional sausages with origins from Moscow to Munich. Fermented products are also a big draw, including *tvorog* (quark), *kefir* (fermented milk) and the low-alcohol drink *kvass*, made with old rye bread. Buy a bit of everything and assemble a novel charcuterie platter. **480 Centre Road, Bentleigh 9557 4028 / Mo–Fr 9am–6pm, Sa 9am–5pm, Su 9am–3pm.**

LEFT Smith & Deli.

Markets

Prahran Market

Prahran Market opened in 1891. Like the rest of Melbourne, it was invigorated by post-war European migrants, who brought then-novel seafood such as sardines and calamari to heritage traders such as Claringbolds, while Pino's started ordering obscure vegetables called "spinach" and "zucchini". With regular appearances by celebrity chefs and a growing coterie of organic traders, it's made a name for itself as the upmarket market.

GARY'S QUALITY MEATS. Since 1975, fourth-generation butcher Gary McBean has been sourcing directly from some of the country's best farms, such as Greta Valley for free-range pork; Gape Grim and Robbins Island for beef; and Flinders Island for lamb. While you might see these brands elsewhere, Gary's sets itself apart with its sleek prism coolroom, where sides of beef are hung to dry-age, tenderising and developing a deeper flavour. Gary's also makes sopressa, kabana and other smallgoods itself.

PADDLEWHEEL. Paddlewheel offers hard-to-find produce from small independent farmers: Seville oranges direct from Margery Welles's family farm, hand-picked silverbeet grown in Mildura, and Pink Fir Apple potatoes grown at Somerset Heritage Produce. There's also a terrific range of Australian-grown organic almonds and sun-dried apricots from Howieson Farm in Koraleigh, fresh milk by Gippsland Jersey and Oak and Swan sourdough from Mardan, South Gippsland.

NAHEDA'S CHOICE. Ghassan and Naheda Hassan have developed a following for the traditional dips and homemade sweets they learned to make in their home country of Lebanon. They make more than 100, including chunky basil and cashew; Kalamata tapenade; and our pick, The Bomb – a mix of garlic aioli, chilli pesto and three types of olives. There's also nougat and mascarpone date creams served in a tiny waffle cone. Visit the second Naheda's outlet for 30 flavours of Turkish delight.

DAMIAN PIKE. It's for people like Damian Pike we go to markets at all. For 30 years, The Mushroom Man has been championing the humble fungus in all its forms – he's even received an Order of Australia for his services. Pike stocks more than 40 varieties and is a rare retail source of wild varieties such as pines and slippery jacks. In winter he stocks local truffles, and when local mushies aren't available, Pike brings in Europe's best from Hungary and pied de moutons from France.

SEE ALSO: Ripe the Organic Grocer (pg.43), Maker & Monger (pg.61), Claringbold's (pg.81), Hagen's Organic Butcher (pg.93), Market Lane (pg.114), The Essential Ingredient (pg.134).

South Melbourne Market

South Melbourne Market started in 1867. That it's survived this long is remarkable – it was bombed in 1981 (no one's quite sure who did it, disgruntled traders or the mafia), then lost two sheds to fire. It's always been a fulcrum for Melbourne's migrant communities – first the Chinese, then post-war Europeans. Some of these traders are still around, contributing to the market's well-rounded feel.

ATYPIC CHOCOLATE. Charles Lemai, Atypic Chocolate's founder and chocolatier, demonstrates his "bean-to-bar" process at this specialist outlet. Atypic imports ethically grown cacao beans from the Solomon Islands, Haiti, Brazil and Madagascar, then blends them with organic milk, raw sugar and non-GMO sunflower lecithin to make single-origin bars in white, dark and milk chocolate varieties. If you have to choose just one, make it the 70 per cent cacao Haiti, which has an earthy, mineral character.

GEORGIE'S HARVEST. At Georgie's Harvest, a potato isn't merely a potato: it's a royal blue, kipfler or viking. Owner Georgie Dragwidge sources between 16 and 25 varieties from Victoria and Tasmania. Each has its selling points, whether it's making the creamiest mash (russet burbank or virginia rose) or having the tastiest skin. Cooks keep coming back for her pumpkins; nuggety little yams; sweet-smelling Australian ginger; log-grown mushrooms; vanilla beans; incendiary habaneros and hard-to-find local wasabi.

AZALEA. Michael Pavlou found his calling early. He wrapped posies at his uncle's florist from the age of 10; worked with his father at the Melbourne wholesale flower markets; and with his stepmum Cherrie Miriklis at Fitzroy's Flowers Vasette. At Azalea he specialises in native arrangements, warm-climate varietals and tropical plants. Because of his deep familial connection to floristry, Pavlou often goes directly to growers, ensuring the freshest possible blooms at the lowest possible prices.

FIELD, BARNS & CO. Few local businesses churn butter right where they sell it. Here, owner Michael Dragwidge (husband of Georgie at Georgie's Harvest) does it with fresh cream from How Now Happy Cow farm near Shepparton. Classic salted and unsalted butters are joined by interpretations such as herb, garlic and parsley. Field, Barns & Co. also stocks 35 varieties of flour, including stone-ground spelt from Birregurra, a green-banana variety and whole-wheat durum for pizza dough.

SEE ALSO: Agathe Patisserie (pg.28), Aptus Seafood (pg.83), T.O.M.S. The Organic Meat Specialist (pg.92), Hagen's Organic Butcher (pg.93), Padre Coffee (pg.112), Tea Drop (pg.112).

A BROADSHEET BOOK

Queen Victoria Market

This is an institution nearly all Melburnians feel connected to. Popping down to the market for shopping and a borek is for many a ritual as universal as going to the footy. Choose from innumerable fruit and vegetable vendors scattered across multiple sheds, or head to the dedicated organic aisle. There's also a vast hall for deli items, and another for meat and fish.

M&G CAIAFA. This bakery has been handing loaves across its marble counter for more than 40 years, and the crowd's still three deep. The corner stall is a bakery aggregator, collecting breads from bakers such as Noisette, Crumbs, 5 & Dime Bagels, Burnham Beeches, Rosie's and Phillippa's. If you're up early there are hot croissants and Kwak scrolls, but if you've slept in there'll still be freshly ground peanut butter and a range of boutique chocolate as consolation.

THE CHICKEN PANTRY. Across the aisle from M&G Caiafa, The Chicken Pantry stocks free-range organic chicken from Barossa and Milawa; ducks from Great Ocean and Mickelham; Mick Durdin's Muscovy and Pekin varieties; and free-range turkey by Deutschers from Dadswell Bridge. If you're trying to source something more unusual, the Chicken Pantry can sort you out with quail (and quail eggs) from the Yarra Valley, plus duck and chicken livers. Other meats include pigeon, kangaroo, rabbit, emu and crocodile.

G&C FRESH PRODUCE. Vic Market's sheer number of grocers with farm-fresh produce defies summation, but G&C Fresh Produce is one of our favourites. Gus and Carmel Bressi have been stall-holders since 1978 and still have some of the best-looking vegetables in the market, from the stark whites of their leek stems, to the fleshy magenta of their beets, all handsomely arranged on hessian sacks and weaved baskets. Gus and Carmel don't believe in coolrooms: their stuff's too fresh.

CURDS & WHEY. This stall is easily identified by its enormous slab of Warrnambool butter, which owner Anne Burley can be seen carving hunks off. Most people, though, are here for the fine local and imported cheeses, which change seasonally. Sometimes you'll see the Woodside Rubi, a soft goat's-milk number covered in flowers. Other times, *barricato al pepe*, a semi-hard Venetian speckled with cracked pepper. Curds also stocks a range of cheese-friendly produce such as passata and balsamic vinegars.

SEE ALSO: Bill's Farm (pg.56), Happy Tuna (pg.81), George the Fishmonger (pg.83), Hagen's Organic Butcher (pg.93), Padre Coffee (pg.112), Market Lane (pg.114).

Flemington Farmers' Market

Flemington Market (established in 2010) mightn't be the biggest or oldest in the city, but it comfortably holds its own against higher-profile markets, not least due to the rotating roster of regulars and seasonal guests, often selling produce from their own farms. The beauty of the farmers' market model is they'll only turn up if their crop is in season. Importantly, dogs are welcome, so long as they don't cause a ruckus.

J&L HOWELL. John Howell sells apples from his 160-year-old orchard in the Yarra Valley, which his forebears planted. He uses an absolute minimum amount of chemicals. In recent years he's been concentrating on heirloom varieties such as the heritage Stuarts planted by his grandfather, and Bramley Seedlings from the 14th century. Howell's pear game is strong, too: try the cara-mel-sweet beurre boscs or buttery winter nelis. In summer there are blood- and yellow-flesh plums, cherries, figs and mulberries.

BENVIEW FARMS. The sheep at Benview live their lives looking out over the Pyrenees Ranges in Western Victoria. Tim and Katherine Pilkington are committed to handling their flock as little as possible, in order to minimise stress. In place of hormones, they concentrate on soil nutrition to raise high quality lambs. Before going to market, Benview lamb is dry-aged for seven days to increase tenderness. You'll find every cut imaginable here – from leg and shoulder to kidney and heart.

REAL FREE RANGE EGGS. Dan the Egg Man was formerly Dan Green, economics honours graduate and longtime independent filmmaker. But Green packed up for Carrajung in the Strzelecki Ranges to raise chooks. His flock of 900 Isa Browns are kept at a stocking ratio of 300 hens per hectare, which they roam at their leisure. They're protected by a battalion of adorable sand-coloured Maremma dogs. None of the birds are debeaked or fed any hormones, antibiotics or grain with artificial colouring.

SPRING CREEK ORGANICS. For the essentials in seasonal veg, Spring Creek Organics sells giant silverbeet and kale; crisp turnips, swedes and celeriac; and luminous purple cauliflower. One of Spring Creek's specialities is its enormous organic daikons, which are a pale cream colour and perfectly suited to light pickling. In spring you'll find heirloom pumpkins, such as the Japanese kabocha that grows well in cooler climates, and the small, striped Brianna with its sweet yellow flesh.

Fishmongers

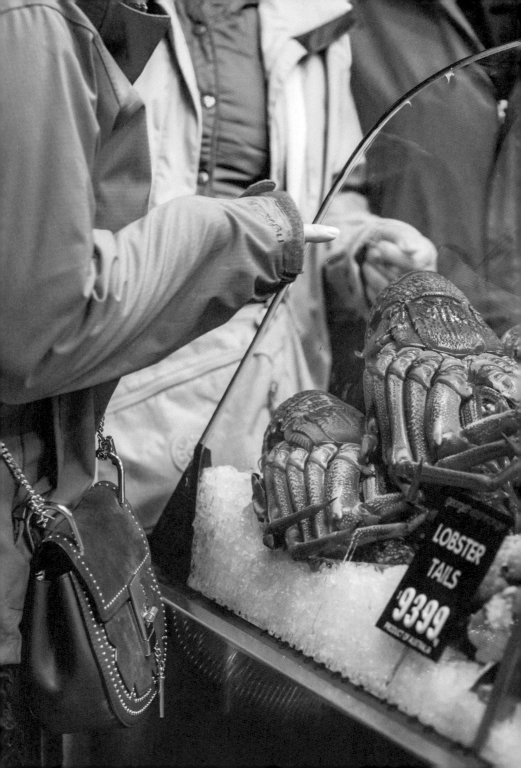

LOBSTER
TAILS
$9399
PRODUCT OF AUSTRALIA

Fishmongers don't typically foster a cult following, but Ocean Made is an exception. Supplying Melbourne's best restaurants is its primary business; you'll spot its fleet of cobalt-blue vans darting from Attica to Estelle, shuttling around 15 tonnes of seafood each week. Fortunately for the non-restaurant-owning public the company has a small retail outlet in a Collingwood laneway. Ocean Made is committed to ethically produced seafood, sourced directly from farms, and also visits Kensington Market before dawn each morning to select wild-caught fish. Along with a greatest-hits selection of salmon and snapper you'll often find slimy mackerel and fresh sardines that go beautifully over a wood fire; blue swimmer crab and enormous green prawns from the Clarence River; line-caught trumpeter from the Bass Strait; Byron Bay spanner crabs and West Australian marron; baby octopus from Lakes Entrance, even whole sea urchin collected off Altona. If what you're after isn't on display, ask your friendly fishmonger – there are three entire warehouses of fish out the back. **27–29 Robert Street, Collingwood / 9486 0399 Tu–Fr 9am–4pm, Sa 8am–2.30pm.**

The Eyes Have It

When buying whole fish, look at the eyes – they should be clear, shiny and plump, not white or discoloured. If you ask, most fishmongers will fillet whole fish for you on the spot.

HAPPY TUNA SEAFOOD

In a market hall where it's hard to make bad choices, Happy Tuna is a Queen Vic (pg.72) go-to. Wayne Chitty and his family have been in this business four generations – his grandfather began working here in the 1920s. Accordingly, those behind the Happy Tuna counter have the answer to almost every conceivable question about seafood and will guide you through the day's produce. Depending on time and the tide, this will likely include excellent sardine fillets, crayfish tail or whole baby snapper straight out of the Bay. There's also a comprehensive source of sustainable, ethically caught and processed seafood, and staff who will happily discuss fishing practices. **Queen Victoria Market Food Court, 513 Elizabeth Street, Melbourne / 9329 7072 / Tu, Th 6am – 2pm, Fr 6am – 5pm, Sa 6am – 3pm, Su 9am – 4pm.**

CLARINGBOLD'S

Claringbold's has been a fixture at Prahran Market (pg.69) since 1909, thanks to its encyclopaedic range of Australian seafood. Visit for South Australian blue swimmer; live scallops collected off Rottnest Island; broadbill swordfish and Spanish mackerel caught in Port Lincoln; banana prawns from the Spencer Gulf; fresh mussels from Spring Bay. There's also a select variety of imports. Our pick? The sashimi-grade Norwegian fjord ocean trout caught in waters fed by the 10,000-year-old Folgefonna glacier – which is exclusive to Claringbold's. It also offers an excellent online delivery service, but turning up in person has its benefits, the in-house sushi counter foremost among them. **Shop 510, Prahran Market, 163–181 Commercial Road, South Yarra / 9826 8381 Tu, Th – Sa 7am – 5pm, Su 10am – 3pm.**

ABOVE Footscray Market. **LEFT** Ocean Made.

POSEIDON SEAFOOD

Strictly speaking, Poseidon Oysters & Seafood is a wholesale business, but those of us without a reason to buy in bulk can still get a taste via the small retail outlet in Fairfield. It specialises in local catch from the waters of Victoria, Tasmania and New Zealand, but is also your go-to for caviar, with a limited selection of imports on the menu. Manager Chris Nicolaidis can hook you up with fresh trevally, snapper, flathead, whiting, dory, blue-eye, flounder, garfish, rainbow trout and rockling. **30 Steane Street, Alphington / 9497 2811 Th & Fr 8am – 4.30pm, Sa 8am – 1.30pm.**

GEORGE THE FISHMONGER

George the Fishmonger is among Vic Market's (pg.72) best suppliers. He's known for his enormous southern rock lobsters (raw or cooked); sashimi-grade yellowfin; fresh pink fillets of wild-caught barramundi; live mud crabs; and Coffin Bay oysters, which he'll shuck on the spot. Got a tricky question? Ask away. George grew up in a family of fishmongers and has been running his own stall at Vic Market for more than a decade. **Shop 35, Meat Hall, Queen Victoria Market, Elizabeth Street, Melbourne / 9329 9642 / Tu, Th 6am – 2pm, Fr 6am – 5pm, Sa 6am – 3pm, Su 9am – 4pm.**

HAI TRIEU SEAFOOD

It makes a lot of sense that Springvale market is one of Attica chef Ben Shewry's personal favourites. One of the most underrated markets in Melbourne, Springvale spills over with Vietnamese, Chinese, Cambodian and Laotian ingredients. At Hai Trieu, you can score giant mud crabs, excellent lobster, oysters, snails and live fish. For an authentic Vietnamese experience, try less conventional molluscs, such as the bailer shells, with their intriguing yellow and orange spots. If you can't figure out what you're looking at – let alone how to cook it – do ask the folks behind the counter, who will help guide you through your purchase. **12/258 Springvale Road, Springvale / 9546 4458 Mo – Su 8am – 6pm.**

D&K LIVE SEAFOOD

D&K is a culinary aquarium, painted blue throughout and stocked with thrashing produce. The large seawater-filled tanks house live South Australian pippies harvested from the wild, and Victorian southern rock lobster. There are also fresh oysters from Coffin Bay in South Australia and St Helens in Tasmania, as well as abalone, urchin, king crab and Balmain bugs from Lakes Entrance. The family-owned shop is at the far end of Leeds Street, a short walk from the station. Look for the lobster logo. **Shop 1 – 3, 28A Leeds Street, Footscray / Mo – Su 8am – 6.30pm.**

M&C SEAFOODS

M&C is one of the state's largest seafood whole-salers, but has a small self-serve outlet where it sells directly to the public. Head to Preston and you'll find whole black tiger prawns and Victorian tuna; fillets of flathead; blue grenadier; ocean trout; octopus; calamari; and smoked salmon and trout. It's also where we head for oysters, with a range of Australia's best that of course includes both Pacific and Sydney rock, which you can take home whole or have shucked on-site. **1 Reserve Street, Preston / 9416 9311 / We – Fr 7.30am – 5pm, Sa 7.30am – 2pm.**

APTUS SEAFOOD

Theo Zahos left the Greek island of Euboea in 1960 and set up Aptus Seafood shortly after. While he still works behind the counter sometimes, his son Angelo is now at the helm, bringing in Tasmanian salmon, fresh prawns, cooked crayfish and sashimi-grade tuna direct from suppliers. You'll find fresh blue swimmers and red mullet, as well as scallops on the half-shell, live abalone and a limited stock of Victorian sea urchins. If you need further motivation, Aptus regularly sells $1 oysters. **Shop 25, South Melbourne Market, Coventry & Cecil Streets, South Melbourne / 9699 7189 We 7am – 4pm, Fr 7am – 5pm, Sa & Su 7am – 4pm.**

LEFT Footscray Market.

Butchers

MEATSMITH

The thing about rare-breed producers is they're, well, rare. Chefs generally get first pick from what can be very limited stock, and the public often barely getting a look in. Not so at Meatsmith, where butcher Troy Wheeler and acclaimed restaurateur Andrew McConnell happily share their connects. Here you'll find top-of-the-line cuts from O'Connor (producers of incredible grass-fed Victorian beef), Yarra Valley's Thousand Candles Wagyu, chooks by Milking Yard in Trentham, dressed Wiltipoll lamb racks and even incredible whole Duroc suckling pig. Wheeler has been in the game two decades and you'll hear a lot of praise for the cold-cuts he makes in-house. That praise is absolutely justified. Choose from duck, pistachio and smoked veal tongue *pate en croute*; house-made mortadella with pork, bacon and pistachios; and the straight-up Wagyu bresaola served at McConnell's Gertrude Street wine bar, Marion. In true McConnell style there's a wide variety of tasteful accoutrements to accompany said meat: pickles and condiments from The Builders Arms; seasonal produce (kipfler potatoes, cippolini onions); a range of knives, and loaves by Baker Bleu (p.28). A smart selection of wine, beer and spirits by former Supernormal sommelier Leanne Altmann renders a bottle shop visit unnecessary. If you can't wait to get your meat-goods home, at the Fitzroy location you can sit in for a Reuben sandwich and glass of Chablis. **273 Smith Street, Fitzroy / 9419 8558 Mo – Sa 9am – 7pm, Su 10am – 5pm. 227A Barkly Street, St Kilda / 9534 3434 / Mo – Sa 9am – 7pm, Su 10am – 5pm.**

BERTIES BUTCHER

This Swan Street shopfront has been a butchery for almost 150 years. The current tenants live up to the expectations of that history by cutting from whole carcasses stored in the anterior coolroom (a surprising rarity). Instead of working with wholesalers, Berties has relationships with individual farmers. Wuk Wuk organic beef comes from Grassvale Farm in East Gippsland, and pork from Greta Valley is delivered by Brian the Farmer every Wednesday. Saltbush lamb is flown in from Flinders Island, and the always-excellent Bannockburn provides free-range chickens. Cold-cuts and deli-style dips are also offered, as are meat-friendly mustards, relishes and wines. **218 Swan Street, Richmond / 9428 2655 / Mo – Fr 7am – 7pm, Sa 8am – 5pm, Su 9am – 5pm.**

PETER BOUCHIER

The sign out the front says "Butcher of Distinction". It fits. Peter Bouchier trades in high-end meat suppliers such as Tasmania's Cape Grim, David Blackmore Wagyu and Glenloth chicken. Frankfurts, weisswurst, kranksy and bratwurst are made to traditional recipes and non-German sausages arrive in configurations such as lamb, spinach and pine nut. Bouchier is also one of the only Australian suppliers of Ireland's Clonakilty Blackpudding Co, which also makes a white variety that doesn't contain blood. Our tip? Buy both. **551 Malvern Road, Toorak / 9827 3629 Mo – Fr 8am – 6pm, Sa 7am – 5pm, Su 9am – 4pm. David Jones Food Hall, 310 Bourke Street, Melbourne / 9643 2530 / Mo – We 10am – 7pm, Th & Fr 10am – 9pm, Sa & Su 9am – 7pm.**

ABOVE Berties Butcher. **LEFT** Meatsmith.

LEON'S SMALLGOODS

Leon's will certainly supply your standard meat needs – mince, chops, steaks and chicken – but this butcher-delicatessen hybrid truly shines with the cured, smoked, salted or pickled. Sliced prosciutto is beautifully marbled, and the handmade salamis and kaiserfleisch are superlative. Leon's Russian and Eastern European section is particularly strong, which is no surprise given the location. **262 Carlisle Street, Balaclava / 9534 2263 / Mo – Fr 8am – 6pm, Sa 8am – 5.30, Su 9am – 5pm.**

LARGO BUTCHER

Following in the footsteps of countless butchers before them, Roger and Simon Ongarato took over Largo from their father. What's less common is that these butchers have their own farm. Beef is hung and dry-aged in-store and regularly sourced from their property. The speckled, buttery Wagyu bresaola and prosciutto are excellent, and Largo is a reliable supplier of rabbit, quail and occasionally goat. **411 Brunswick Street, Fitzroy / 9417 268 Mo – Sa 9am – 5pm.**

SKINNER & HACKETT

Gerald's Bar is where chefs like to eat – with good reason. Owner Gerald Diffey knows where to find the best produce and most importantly, not to mess with it. Lucky for us, that produce is sold at the butcher-slash-provedore next door. There's Mirboo chicken; dry-aged beef; Three Rivers saltbush lamb and Borrowdale free-range pork. Behind the counter is Jonathan Stobbs, whose enthusiasm for quality meat is barely contained. Have a chat with him: you're guaranteed to learn something. **400 Rathdowne Street, Carlton / 9347 6642 Mo – Fr 10am – 7pm, Sa & Su 10am – 6pm.**

HUDSON MEATS

In just 10 years Hudson Meats has become one of Sydney's finest butchers. While less well known in Melbourne, its reputation is growing. The slogan here is "nose-to-tail", and so-called secondary cuts, such as shoulder, are given pride of place. The butcher has relationships with individual farmers and stocks Gippsland Beef and Kyneton's Piper Street Food Co. charcuterie – look for the duck and pistachio terrine. It's also home to the maligned but entirely tasty haggis. **459 Toorak Road, Toorak / 9827 7711 / Mo – Fr 9am – 7pm, Sa & Su 9am – 5pm.**

DONATI'S FINE MEATS

Leo Donati's appreciation of classical opera is legendary – walk into his shop and you might hear Puccini's *Turandot*. Bench tops are polished marble, and an Ivan Durrant oil painting of a pig's head hangs on the wall. Given Donati's love for the old country, it's unsurprising his heart lies with Italian cuisine. You'll find osso bucco and polpette alongside acquired tastes such as ox tongue, and there's a fridge full of smallgoods. **402 Lygon Street, Carlton / 9347 4948 / Mo 6.30am – 6pm, Tu – Fr 7am – 6pm, Sa 6am – 1pm.**

NINO'S & JOE'S

Nino Agnesi began his apprenticeship in 1968 at age 15. Accordingly, Nino and Joe's is a traditional butcher shop. Biodynamic and organic aren't watchwords here; it's about quality cuts taken from whole beasts out back. But the main reason you're here is the handmade sausages, which are squeezed out thick and thin, in pork and fennel or casalingo varieties. **317 Victoria Street, Brunswick / 9380 2081 / Tu – Fr 6am – 5.30pm, Sa 6am – 12.30pm.**

RIGHT Gary's Quality Meats.

CANNINGS FREERANGE BUTCHER

As the name suggests, this butcher specialises in free-range produce. Products are raised without growth hormones or antibiotics and are not genetically modified, but suppliers aren't certified organic – the rationale here is that Cannings's farmers can reduce the final cost of ethically produced pasture-fed meat if they don't have to pay certification fees. Nevertheless, producers have excellent credentials: Large White Cross Landrace pigs come from the Darling Downs; Victorian beef is both grass fed and finished (as opposed to grass-raised, then sent to a grain feedlot before slaughter, as can be the case). Cannings also supports the Humane Society, Animals Australia and the Marine Conservation Society. **195 Glenferrie Road, Malvern / 1300 513 623 / Mo – Sa 7am – 7pm, Su 10am – 7pm. Other locations: Hawthorn, Ivanhoe, Kew, South Yarra, Tooronga.**

T.O.M.S. THE ORGANIC MEAT SPECIALIST

Originally a wholesale-only organic butcher, Tom Niall decided he wanted to get a little closer to the eaters of his meat (and perhaps "The Organic Meat Specialist" was too convenient an acronym to pass up). Now, the T.O.M.S. stall in South Melbourne Market (pg.70) acts as a conduit between free-range farmers and discerning cooks. There's saltbush lamb from Remarkable Meat Co. in South Australia, and from Victoria, biodynamically grown Wagyu from the Western District and rare-breed Berkshire pigs from the foothills of the Warby Ranges. Basil, rosemary and lamb burgers and pork Cumberland sausages are made in-house. For the more game, order partridge, quail, goat, venison or pheasant. **Shop 30, Deli Aisle, South Melbourne Market, Corner Cecil and Coventry Streets, South Melbourne / 9699 7926 / We 7am – 4pm, Fr 7am – 5pm, Sa & Su 7am – 4pm.**

Hagen's, founded in 1999, was one of Melbourne's first biodynamic and hormone-free butchers. At every one of its stores you'll find grass-fed, dry-aged Angus; organic Wagyu; organic saltbush lamb; Berkshire pork; nitrate-free hams and bacon; and house-made snags. Hagen's has relationships with the state's best producers, including McIvor Farm in Tooborac, which raises Berkshire pigs that spend their entire lives foraging outside. Rose veal (from older calves) comes from Mac's Creek in the Otway Ranges, where John and Anne Boyd use natural compost from their dairy farm to improve pastures. Chooks are sourced from Milking Yard in Trentham, where rare-breed Sommerlad chickens are guarded by border collies Henry and Gus. If you're overwhelmed by choice, or looking for something special, your best bet is simply to have a chat. These butchers know their stuff and are happy to share. Past that, you can book in for a butchery lesson in the dedicated classroom. **52 Lennox Street, Richmond / 9428 2471 / Mo – Fr 5am – 4pm. Other locations: Bentleigh, South Melbourne Market, Queen Victoria Market, Prahran Market.**

Rest. Your. Meat.

Not just after cooking, but before, too. Whether it's beef, lamb, pork, poultry or game, taking large pieces out of the fridge an hour before you expose it to heat will ensure the meat cooks evenly, and helps avoid a cold-spot in the middle.

ABOVE AND LEFT Hagen's Organic Butcher.

Kid-Friendly Food

with JAMIE *&* LOREN McBRIDE

The McBride's make entertaining look easy. It helps that hospitality appears to be in their DNA. Both grew up in restaurant families and now have a string of venues to their names including Mammoth, Primo and Gilson. But regardless of their experience, no one with one- and two-year-old children (let alone several restaurants) has time to burn.

For Jamie and Loren, making lunch for friends means making it a kid-friendly adventure: a trip to Prahran Market and a Lebanese-themed barbeque cooked by the whole family (both their fathers are Lebanese). "It's a really easy, stress-free option, and it's generally enjoyed by kids as well," Loren says. "The market becomes like an outing for us, and I love it because we go on a Tuesday when they have a petting zoo, or we go on a Thursday when the music man's there."

The McBrides shop at Pino's in Prahran Market (pg.69), which has great produce and servers who will select and box it up for you. "It's the grocer we always go to," Loren says. "He feeds the kids fruit while I'm shopping, it's perfect."

Like the rest of us, two-year-old Fred is entranced by the selection at Gary's Quality Meats (pg.69). "If we're entertaining we will get some lamb and make kofta," Loren says.

"Fred's a very adventurous little boy and doesn't do what I tell him to do most of the time. Finding ways to keep him entertained is important. Getting him involved in the process is the best way to do that. He loves to grab his little stepladder. I give him a blunt knife and his own chopping board, and he'll chop away with me, or attempt to," Loren says.

Sweets

Cocoa butter tends to pick up the smell of whatever it's stored near – so keep chocolate wrapped and away from smelly onions. Good chocolate keeps best airtight in the pantry, away from sunlight and moisture.

PIDAPIPÓ

Gelato University is a real thing. It's in Anzola dell'Emilia, near Bologna, and Lisa Valmorbida is a graduate. Her expertise will be obvious to anyone who's had a spoonful at Pidapipó. All products are made daily, using ingredients that skew local unless quality demands imports: pistachios from Sicily, hazelnuts from Piedmont, milk from Warrnambool, cheese from St Kilda's La Formaggeria and honey from a hive on the roof. Next is the method by which the gelato is stored. It doesn't much like the heat and air exposure it gets in typical glass display cases, so Pidapipó keeps its ice-cream in *pozettis*, Italian-designed insulated pots that keep the temperature consistent and allow the gelato to be churned without adding stabilisers. There's one last reason you'll find a queue outside Pidapipó, regardless of season. Along with traditional flavours such as zabaglione, tiramisu, mint choc-chip, pistachio, hazelnut and chocolate, Valmorbida and her team are constantly mixing up something more experimental but no less delicious – lavender and lemon sorbetto, say, or coconut rice pudding with swirled rhubarb coulis, or bush-wattle cream. Inventiveness and impeccable taste are skills no university can teach. **299 Lygon Street, Carlton / 9347 4596 / Mo – Su 12pm – 11pm. 85 Chapel Street, Windsor / 9224 1938 / Mo – Su 12pm – 11pm.**

ABOVE Pidapipó. **RIGHT** Cobb Lane.

COBB LANE

Cobb Lane's Matt Forbes has made pastry at such establishments as the two-Michelin-starred Le Manoir Aux Quat' Saisons, Shannon Bennett's Vue de Monde, Gordon Ramsay's Maze and a little-known place in Copenhagen called Noma. Despite the lofty credentials, Forbes simply likes to make doughnuts. And we like to eat them: irregular ovals of mid-weight pastry, filled with lemon and lime curd, apple crumble or rosewater custard. While the doughnuts are compulsory, try some of Forbes's lesser-hyped pleasures: a kouign-amann cake made with croissant pastry and filled with pistachio butter, or a salted caramel and cardamom Oreo. **13 Anderson Street, Yarraville 9687 1538 / Mo – Fr 7.30am – 4.30pm, Sa – Su 8.30am – 4.30pm.**

DOUGHBOY DOUGHNUTS

For a long time, doughnuts came in two flavours: jam, and cinnamon and sugar. Then Doughboys came along with banoffee pie, lime toast, strawberry panna cotta and dozens of other combinations. Ten are available here each day, crowning chubby rings or piped inside misshapen balls. The dough is always the lighter, yeasty, American style, as opposed to the denser French *beignet*. We can't recommend a specific flavour given how often they change – just know that everything is done on-site to exacting standards. If your doughnut has a brownie crumbled over it, the brownie has been mixed and baked right there in the busy open kitchen. **535 Bourke Street, Melbourne / Mo – Fr 7am – 4.30pm, Sa 9am – 4pm.**

BALHA'S PASTRY

Balha makes a strong case for Melbourne's best baklava. It bakes the Lebanese style, which is drier than Turkish versions. What sets baker Tarik Afiouni's apart is the quality of his ghee and the freshness of his pistachios, which are Australian-grown whenever possible. You should also sample the orange-blossom-infused *fatira*, or a slice of *knefeh*, a Beirut-style cheesecake. Fasting during Ramadan is made that little bit easier knowing Balha's is making *karabij* – a traditional semolina cake. **761–763 Sydney Road, Brunswick 9383 3944 / Mo–Su 9am–11pm**

PANA CHOCOLATE

Pana Barbounis and his staff hand-make every bar from raw Amazonian cacao, with no added sugar. The vegan-friendly bars are earthy and gritty, with a gratifying tang. They're made right on-site, alongside truffles, ganache, fudge, cookies, lamingtons, cream-pops and brownies. Don't leave without a signature Vespa Wheel: a buckwheat wafer biscuit with a coconut mallow centre and raspberry-chia jam. It'll make you wonder why you ever liked Wagons. **491 Church Street, Richmond / 1300 717 488 / Mo–Fr 10.30am–5pm, Sa 10.30am–4pm, Su 11am–4pm.**

KOKO BLACK

When Shane Hills started Koko Black in 2003, he went straight to the world's chocolate capital to find his chocolatier. That person (Dries Cnockaert) may have gone home to Bruges, but his legacy lives through current chocolatiers who combine Belgian expertise with great Australian ingredients such as Bakery Hill whisky, Tasmanian leatherwood, and walnuts from Ballarat. Try a yuzu truffle; a dark pistachio; amango and vanilla; a rose jelly; and whatever else catches your eye. **52 Collins Street, Melbourne / 9663 5567 / Mo–Fr 8.30am–6pm, Sa 10am–6pm, Su 11am–6pm. Other locations: Carlton, Chadstone Shopping Centre, Westfield Doncaster, Highpoint Shopping Centre, Queen Victoria Market, Royal Arcade Melbourne.**

DOLCETTI

Thanks to her Sicilian-born mother and time at Baker D. Chirico, Dolcetti's Marianna Di Bartolo knows her way around a custard *bombolone*. She makes everything from scratch, just like her mother taught – from the pistachio and sour cherry amaretti, to the cultishly popular nougat. The florentines deserve your attention for their arrangement of coffee-coloured almonds, candied orange and the occasional cherry encased in dark chocolate. **223 Victoria Street, West Melbourne 9328 1688 / Tu 8.30am–3.30pm, Th–Sa 8.30am –3.30pm, Su 9am–3pm.**

BEATRIX

Nat Paull has baked in the kitchens of Stephanie Alexander, Maggie Beer, Greg Malouf and Cath Claringbold, which explains the homey counter at Beatrix. There's not a delicately assembled gateaux in sight. Apple custard crumble tarts are pleasingly uneven, and her banana pecan butter cake is served in large wedges. Paull is an artist when it comes to the sponge, with cloud-like layers concealing an inland sea of creme fraiche and blood-orange curd. Beauty is only icing-deep. **688 Queensberry Street, North Melbourne Tu–Sa 9am–4pm.**

LA BELLE MIETTE

Remember when the entire city seemed obsessed with macarons? Bite into one of these delicate meringue sandwiches and you'll understand why. Patissier Maylynn Tsoi doesn't go for elaborate combinations – she picks a couple of unconventional yet complementary flavours. Hits include cherry blossom and sake; ginger and macadamia; and for Mother's Day, Belgian chocolate and Piper-Heidsieck champagne. Present a friend with a Kano Hollamby-designed box and you'll be in their good books for months. **30 Hardware Lane, Melbourne / 9024 4528 / Mo–Th 10am–6pm, Fr 10am–9pm, Sa 10am–5pm, Su 10am–4pm. Other locations: Richmond, Collins Street (Melbourne), Chadstone Shopping Centre.**

RIGHT T Cavallaro & Sons.

T. CAVALLARO & SONS

Rolled out by hand, passed through a granite refiner, curled into a loose tube and deep-fried until they blister. Yes, the cannoli at T. Cavallaro and Sons are simple. When you put in your order they're piped to the point of over-filling with vanilla and chocolate patisserie cream or whipped ricotta, marsala and almonds. It's a Cavallaro-family recipe that hasn't changed since Tomasso emigrated from Lipari in 1956, and continues to be followed daily by sons Tony and Carmelo. **98 Hopkins Street, Footscray / 9687 4638 / Mo–Fr 8.30am–5pm, Sa 8am–4pm, Su 8am–12pm.**

Coffee & Tea

Grind As You Go

Coffee oxidises just like wine, so keep whole beans in an airtight container. Ground coffee goes off quicker, so invest in an at-home grinder.

TEA DROP

Tea Drop was founded in 2005 by Sri Lankan-born entrepreneur Ashok Dias, but it was almost a decade before its first physical brew-bar arrived at South Melbourne Market. Here you can sample well over 100 blends. Try a white tea from China aged 10 years; a Japanese sencha grown on the mountains of Shizuoka, Japan; or an antioxidant-packed Golden Tips Pu Erh. All teas are ethically sourced and seasonally hand-picked from small producers. **Shop 34, South Melbourne Market, corner of Cecil and Coventry Streets 9383 2300 / We 8am–4pm, Fr 8am–5pm, Sa & Su 8am–4pm.**

PADRE COFFEE

Padre started in 2008, as a small cafe roasting for itself. Now a not-so-small roaster, it has broadened its reach to three further locations in Melbourne and one in Noosa. The original cafe still gives the premiere experience, and that's where you should head. The team sources from up to 30 estates globally for its blends and single origins, including less-common spots such as Indonesia and India. There's a laudable range of brew paraphernalia for sale as well. **438–440 Lygon Street, Brunswick East / 9381 1881 / Mo–Sa 7am–4pm, Su 8am–4pm. Other locations: South Melbourne Market, Melbourne.**

MÖRK CHOCOLATE BREW HOUSE

In a city that lives for coffee, Mörk's singular obsession with hot chocolate is refreshing. Since 2012 founders Josefin Zernell and Kiril Shaginov have been out to prove chocolate can be just as nuanced and interesting as its more-popular cousin. After tasting their range of just-add-milk powders, we have to agree. Take home the Original Dark blend with intense notes of red berries, or a cold dark-chocolate milk bottled in collaboration with St David's Dairy. **150 Errol Street, North Melbourne / 9328 1386 / Tu–Su 9am–5pm.**

A BROADSHEET BOOK

PLUG NICKEL

This cafe doesn't roast its own coffee, but it's one of the few places in Melbourne sourcing beans from Canberra's ONA, owned by 2015 World Barista Champion Sasa Sestic. Pick up a bag of filter roast or Raspberry Candy, the espresso blend that won Sestic his award. Plug Nickel also makes and sells its own Indian-style chai to take home. There's a range of free, easy-to-follow leaflets to guide you through various brew methods, including espresso, filter and French press. 7 **Peel Street, Collingwood / 9416 3677 Mo – Fr 7am – 4pm, Sa 8am – 4pm, Su 9am – 4pm.**

AUNTY PEG'S

This HQ for Proud Mary's is truly uncompromising – no milk is allowed on premises. But go with it. Before choosing your beans, taste a brew from one of three group heads hacked out of an espresso machine and installed in the central bar like beer taps. The Proud's team is particularly interested in how processing changes a coffee: an El Salvadorian Bourbon varietal comes three different ways – washed, natural and in an experimental "glazed" technique. **200 Wellington Street, Collingwood / 9417 1333 / Mo – Fr 8am – 5pm.**

MAKER FINE COFFEE

This roaster was founded in 2014 by Stephanie Manolas and John Vroom, who's logged time at Liar Liar and Proud Mary. He also won the Victorian Siphon Championship. In a few short years Maker has developed relationships with producers such as the Harries family on the Thika Plateau in Kenya, whose Oreti Estate has been growing coffee for more than 100 years. This is the place to buy these and other high quality beans roasted using the latest technology. **47 North Street, Richmond 9037 4065 / Mo – Fr 7am – 3pm, Sa 8am – 3pm.**

ASSEMBLY

Chrissie Trabucco and Ollie Mackay have followed clean lines to their inescapable conclusion at Assembly, a minimalist temple to coffee and tea. At any one time the cafe and shop stocks about 12 rare and unusual black and green leaves from China, Japan and Taiwan. You'll find delicate "first flush" teas picked at the beginning of the season and pearls of jasmine bloom rolled by hand. The team also dispenses invaluable brewing advice and the equipment you need to make use of it at home. Filter and espresso coffees are roasted at Bureaux Collective, including Ethiopian beans traded through a community exchange; and a Kenyan roast redolent of tangelo and nectarine. Make sure to have an espresso while you shop for something to take home. **60 Pelham Street, Carlton / Mo – Fr 7am – 4pm, Sa 8.30am – 4pm.**

MARKET LANE

Since launching in 2009, Market Lane has been dead set on transparency. Owners Jason Scheltus, Fleur Studd and her father Will (of *Cheese Slices* TV fame) want you to know who grew your coffee and exactly where. They're well placed to tell you – their import arm, Melbourne Coffee Merchants, brings in high-grade green beans for both Market Lane and many other roasters. Over time, the team has developed relationships with some of the best growers in the best growing regions. The nerve-centre of Market Lane's five-strong family of cafes is at the Prahran Market (pg.69), where beans are roasted. **Shop 13, Prahran Market, Elizabeth Street, South Yarra / 9804 7434 / Mo & We 7am – 4pm, Tu & Th – Sa 7am – 5pm, Su 8am – 5pm. Other locations: Queen Victoria Market, Melbourne, Carlton, South Melbourne.**

SEVEN SEEDS

Mark Dundon sparked Melbourne's independent roasting scene. After founding Ray's Cafe and St ALi (both sold), he started Seven Seeds with business partner Bridget Amor. At a time when Melbourne was dominated by dark-roasted, untraceable, commodity-grade beans tailored for espresso, the duo began pushing quality, provenance and lighter roasts to suit filter, cold drip and other brewing styles. They remain some of the best at it. Nowadays roasting happens at a warehouse in Fairfield. Stop in at the Carlton cafe for a professionally brewed cup, then grab a bag of the Golden Gate Espresso blend to replicate that classic cocoa and toffee profile at home. When you brew you'll be making a cup of Melbourne history. **114 Berkeley Street, Carlton / 9347 8664 / Mo – Sa 7am – 5pm, Su 8am – 5pm. Other locations: Melbourne (Traveller, Brother Baba Budan), Docklands (Hortus).**

SMALL BATCH

Andrew Kelly's melding of Nordic chic with Melbourne style was clearly visible in his landmark cafe Auction Rooms, and later in his short-lived CBD brew-bar, Filter. But it's most clearly expressed in his roasting. He began with a humble coffee cart and Kelly now runs one of the world's most respected roasting operations. Following in the footsteps of Norwegian Tim Wendelboe (the closest thing to a rockstar the coffee world has produced), Small Batch coffees are generally lightly roasted and clean, emphasising the inherent floral, fruity and citrus characteristics. Buy a bag of the signature Candyman espresso blend or try one of the excellent single origins. **Auction Rooms, 103 – 107 Errol Street, North Melbourne / 9326 7749 / Mo – Fr 7am – 5pm, Sa & Su 7.30am – 5pm.**

RIGHT Assembly.

Bottle Shops

BLACKHEARTS & SPARROWS

Reliable, affordable, interesting and everywhere. This Victorian bottle-shop chain is run by siblings Paul and Jessica Ghaie and their team of friendly staff members, who will help familiarise you with Australia's great modern winemakers – producers such as Patrick Sullivan, Ochota Barrels, A. Rodda, Lucy Margaux, William Downie and Gentle Folk. You might even meet them if they're in-store to offer tastings. There's also a substantial selection of intriguing international bottles, both from big winemaking nations such as France, Italy and Spain, and also countries less commonly found in Australian bottle shops, such as Greece, Croatia and Georgia. Not everything's boutique, though. Plenty of bottles ring up at less than $20, and there's a dedicated Blackhearts "Gated" range, made in collaboration with local producers, that's priced from $10 to $15. Also in the fridges: canned and bottled beers ranging from the approachable slab to crafty one-offs, say, an Oskar Blues Hotbox Coffee IPA from Colorado. Spirits are particularly select – you'll find high-end gins from Patient Wolf and Four Pillars, Japanese Nikka whisky, and Maidenii vermouth. **113–115 Scotchmer Street, Fitzroy North / 9489 5945 / Mo 11am–8pm, Tu–Fr 11am–9pm, Sa 10am–9pm, Su 10am–8pm. Other locations: Brunswick, East Brunswick, Fitzroy, Kensington, Richmond, Windsor, St Kilda East.**

ABOVE Blackhearts & Sparrows. **RIGHT** City Wine Shop.

CITY WINE SHOP

This bottle-o and restaurant is by the same people who brought you the businesses that surround it: The European, Supper Club and Siglo. As such, City Wine Shop is a compendium of life's finer offerings. Some of those things are made in Europe – say, the house champagne, Champagne Doyard, imported exclusively from the village of Vertus in the Côte des Blancs, from a family with wine-making history back to 1677. Take home a sunny chardonnay Les Prêtres de Quintaine from Viré-Clessé, or sit down for a glass of Dr Timo Mayer's superb Yarra Valley pinot noir. **159 Spring Street, Melbourne / 9654 6657 / Mo & Tu 7am – 11pm, We – Fr 7am – 12am, Sa 9am – 12am, Su 9am – 11pm.**

CULT OF THE VINE

Cult of the Vine is an expression of one man's taste. That man is Brad Lucas, former sommelier at the Lake House in Daylesford, and his taste is impeccable. He offers a broad selection of low-intervention, small-vineyard bottles from Australia, France, Italy, Germany, Portugal and Spain. Our pick is a bottle of Beechworth's best gamay from Sorrenberg, or try a wacky organic from south-west France's Château Lestignac. There's a small selection of craft beer, but wine is the main event. By all means stay for a glass and a hard-boiled egg; Lucas is happy to open most things, within reason. **7 Florence Street, Brunswick / 9383 1542 / Tu – Su 12pm – 9pm.**

OTTER'S PROMISE

Dan Taranto gives beer the respect it deserves. His store stocks 400 brews and its very name is a combination of Maris Otter and Golden Promise, two of the best malts for brewing. Bonus: this is one of a growing number of bottle shops that encourage drinking-in. If you're up for it, try a giant can of Modus Operandi's Gadzooks! IPA with its pineapple-y hops, or an Anagram Blueberry Cheesecake Stout, which tastes just like it says on the label. **1219 High Street, Armadale / Tu & We 12pm–8pm, Th 12pm–9pm, Fr & Sa 12pm–11pm, Su 12pm–8pm.**

PENNY YOUNG

The Bongiovanni families have been Melbourne provedores for generations. Anthony, the latest Bongiovanni in the business, is making his mark with Penny Young, a bottle shop with more than 400 beers. The best names in Australian brewing are represented – such as Feral and La Sirène – as are limited-edition small-batch brews, including Hargreaves Hill Phoenix Imperial Red Ale and Moon Dog's Black Lung VII smoky stout. **22 Young Street, Moonee Ponds / 9326 2999 Mo–Th 9am–7pm, Fr 9am–8pm, Sa 9am–7pm, Su 12am–6pm.**

HARRY & FRANKIE

Wine should be fun. It is at Harry & Frankie, where another former Lake House sommelier, Tom Hogan, actively encourages customers to try something new. Perhaps a gamay by Herve Souhat, or a single-vineyard Syrahmi La La from Heathcote. There are more than 600 varieties on the shelves, so finding something new is easy. You're welcome to take it away, and equally welcome to sit for a few glasses in the Foolscap Studio-designed space. **317 Bay Street, Port Melbourne / 9645 4414 / We & Th 4pm–11pm, Fr–Su 11am–11pm.**

THE ALPS WINE SHOP & BAR

This wine shop and bar has 400 bottles in stock, many available by the glass. Some are biodynamic New World boozes, some traditional Grand Cru, and there's a particular focus on the Jura, Savoie and Burgundy regions at the foothills of the European Alps. The uniting theme is transparency – wines must taste of where they're from. It's the same at sister venues Toorak Cellars, Milton Wine Shop, The Moon and The Hills. **64 Commercial Road, Prahran / 9529 4988 / Mo & Tu 12pm–9pm, We–Su 12pm–11pm.**

PRINCE WINE STORE

This outstanding retailer keeps 4000 lines in stock, concentrating on hard-to-find wines of the classical persuasion. There's a strong emphasis on the Old World, but Australian producers are well represented. Treat yourself to a bottle of Giaconda if your wallet can take it. If not, there are good-value bottles such as Fighting Gully Road chardonnay. There's also 1000 beers and a boutique spirits section. Thanks to in-store wine bar Belotta, you're not even obliged to go home. **177 Bank Street, South Melbourne / 3686 3033 / Mo–Th 10am–8pm, Fr 10am–9pm, Sa 10am–7pm. 80 Primrose Street, Essendon / 9370 6561 / Mo–Th, Sa 10am–8pm, Fr 10am–9pm, Su 12pm–6pm.**

ARMADALE CELLARS

This imposing, double-storey Victorian terrace has been a wine shop since 1997. It's a fitting home for the many bottles from longstanding Australian and European wineries, such as Henschke in the Eden Valley, Mount Mary in the Yarra Valley and France's Dom Perignon. There's a limited selection from younger winemakers, but if you're after new wave or natural wines, you'd be better served heading down the road to Milton Wine Store. Here, owner Phil Hude loves to share his knowledge, whether that means pouring you a few glasses when you walk in, or putting you through a five-week appreciation course in the cellar. **813–817 High Street Armadale / 9509 3055 / Mo–Sa 10am–8pm.**

LEFT The Alps Wine Shop & Bar.

B en Carwyn is a man of vision. When life gave him a regular
suburban bottle shop, he saw an endless plain of craft
beer, single-malt whisky and top-shelf mezcal. There are
well over 250 iterations of whisk(e)y at Carwyn Cellars.
For a mere $600, become the proud owner of a 32-year-old
1983 Adelphi Limited Teaninich, or buy a Starward Solera
from Port Melbourne for under $100. Bottled beers traverse
the alphabet from Abbaye des Rocs Blonde to Wildflower
Gold Australian Wild Ale (no Zs, at time of writing). Carwyn
and his manager Ben Duval both grew up on wineries and
maintain a small, fast-moving selection of wine in the side
room. Carwyn also foresaw that you mightn't want to leave
his cellar, so there's a bar out back with rotating kegs and
vermouth on tap. **877 High Street, Thornbury / 9484 1820**
Su & Mo 12pm – 10pm, Tue – Sa 10am – 11pm.

Decanting: Three Solid Reasons

"The first", says Kisume sommelier Kieran Clarkin, is sedimentation – to avoid that sludgy last glass. The second is to oxygenate the wine and develop its flavour. The third? "It looks cool."

CLOUDWINE CELLARS

Cloudwine began online with an emphasis on small and family-run vignerons. These days, its bricks-and-mortar store stocks about 850 Australian wines. Our highlights from the densely packed shelves include Torzi Matthew's Schist Rock shiraz from Barossa; an award-winning pinot from Barwon Ridge in Geelong and the guava-inflected Freycinet chardonnay. If you're after something from the Northern Hemisphere, head down the adjacent Wynyard Street to find 600 bottles at sister shop, European Wine Store. Cloudwine also has 100 beers in the fridge, mainly focusing on seasonal releases. The concise selection of spirits includes bottles from Tasmania's Belgrove and South Australia's Applewood. **Clarendon Street, South Melbourne / 9699 6700 / Mo – Sa 10am – 8pm, Su 11am – 8pm.**

SAMUEL PEPYS

This Westgarth store was put together by Shane Barrett, Jesse Gerner and Kelly O'Loghlen, part of the team behind restaurants Bomba and Nomada. A retail front for Barrett's import business focussing on Spain and France, the store holds more than 400 wines and 200 spirits from small producers, with a particular focus on sustainable, biodynamic and low-intervention wine. Try the standout Vale da Capucha, a certified organic wine from the Lisbon coast. You'll also find bottles from interesting locals such as Patrick Sullivan, Polperro and Jamsheed, as well as a can't-fail house-bottled Negroni. You'll also find around 10 bottles open to sample at any given time. **96 High Street, Northcote 9481 2449 / Mo – Su 12pm – 9pm.**

ABOVE Blackhearts & Sparrows.

A Set Table

with PASCALE GOMES-McNABB

Pascale Gomes-McNabb is responsible for some of Melbourne's best restaurant interiors. Cumulus Inc. and Stokehouse City have all benefitted from her sharp eye. But her work doesn't necessarily reflect her personal aesthetic. "You need to have an orderliness in a restaurant, and be quite precise," she says. At home she likes a more scattered and eclectic style, rather than one clean look.

"The things that I have in the house are from all over the place. They're things I've bought, found, or been given. They all have special memories," she says. Her approach shows that matching sets of tableware aren't necessarily all that. Interesting pieces selected with thought can make anything work. The plates may be mismatched, but they're all carefully chosen – napery is picked for how it feels in hand, and a rubber rat isn't out of place. "I actually hate live rats, but I really like him," she says. She likes the table to feel intimate and busy when entertaining friends, and sits people close together. "I once sat 18 people round this 10-seat table," she says.

127

"I like to shop at shops, not online," says Gomes-McNabb, "places like Make, Cibi, Nest, Safari Living." TABLE AND WOODEN TRAYS: Arteveneta. CUTLERY: George Jensen. GREEN GLASSES: Upcycled from San Pellegrino bottles by Mark Douglass. BLUE AND WHITE JAPANESE PLATES: Made in Japan. (pg.136) TONGS: Cibi. OTHER CROCKERY: Junk Company. WINE GLASSES: Cedar Hospitality. (pg.136)

Cook & Tableware

THE ESSENTIAL INGREDIENT

The name says it all. If a recipe calls for native pepperberries, sea lettuce or goose fat and nothing else will do, The Essential Ingredient may well have the answer. It stocks hundreds of common and obscure products, from genuine Canadian maple syrup to dried guajillo chillies. That's one part of its appeal. The other is high-quality cookware, tableware and even a few gardening tools. Le Creuset casserole dishes in all colours make the perfect gift. Ditto for sets of Laguiole cutlery and sorbet-coloured ceramics by Mud (pg.136). There's also an overnight knife-sharpening service that pops up once a fortnight. **32 Elizabeth Street, South Yarra / 9827 9047 Tu, Th & Fr 9am–5pm, We 10am–4pm, Sa 8am–5pm, Su 10am–4pm. 266 Coventry Street, South Melbourne / 9827 9047 / Tu 10am–4pm, We–Sa 9am–5pm, Su 10am–4pm.**

DINOSAUR DESIGNS

Dinosaur Designs is an Australian icon. Each piece of brightly coloured or semi-transparent resin feels as though it's made for the hand – certainly, it's made by it. Louise Olsen's sketches are shaped by in-house sculptors, then moulded and buffed to a translucent finish by human beings. It's been this way since 1985, when the three founders began selling polymer-clay jewellery at Sydney's Paddington Markets. As such, Dinosaur Designs makes the most reliable gifts: if you've already got a bone-textured serving spoon or coral-tinted vase, no two will ever be exactly the same. **Shop 6, The Strand, 250 Elizabeth Street, Melbourne / 9650 8000 / Mo–Th 10am–6pm, Fr 10am–8pm, Sa 10am–6pm, Su 11am–5pm. 562 Chapel Street, South Yarra / 9827 2600 Mo–Sa 10am–6pm, Su 11am–5pm.**

ABOVE AND RIGHT Meatsmith.

Whether you're on the lookout for hand-thrown ceramics, or eyeing-off a Corvette-red Kitchenaid, Chef's Hat is the place to get it. Since 1996, chefs, bartenders and passionate amateurs have been visiting this kitchenware retailer opposite South Melbourne Market (pg.70). The range is truly enormous. If you need a fondant smoother, there's one by Cake Boss. A dedicated caviar box? You're sorted. Want a bluetooth-enabled sous vide circulator? We all do. Less esoteric items are available too, of course: irregular stoneware bowls by Churchill; broad-lipped champagne coupes from RCR; bone-coloured Jean Neron cutlery, each embossed with its handsome little bee. For the kitchen itself you'll find cast-iron skillets by American heroes Lodge; dedicated omelette pans by Le Creuset; giant paella pans; high-sided woks; fast-heating cast-aluminium saucepans from Per Forza; and blue-rimmed enamel pie dishes for less than $10. Naturally, there's a whole section devoted to knives: Japanese-forged Sakai Jikko chefs knives; classic Wüsthof German steel; fish-scalers and oyster-shuckers; wood-handled cheese-shaving garrottes; and handcrafted champagne sabres – the ultimate gift. **131 Cecil Street, South Melbourne 9682 1441 / Mo – Fr 9am – 5.30pm, Sa 9am – 4pm, Su 10am – 4pm.**

Sharp Focus

Tanto, Chef's Armoury and many local butchers will enliven your knives, but Meatsmith's Troy Wheeler recommends the Knife Shop on Wellington Street, Collingwood, for its singular focus. "All they do is sharpen knives."

GUILD OF OBJECTS

Three local potters started Guild of Objects in mid-2015. It's part gallery and part collaborative workshop, conveniently aggregating some of the best work by Melbourne makers, including that of founders Brooke Thorn, Chela Edmunds and Tao Oudomvilay. Pieces include mugs, platters, jugs, bowls and other tableware. All are highly individual, featuring irregular shapes, visible finger-prints and clear brush marks where glazes were applied. Pore over your purchases with a brioche doughnut at Beatrix next door. **690 Queensberry Street, North Melbourne / We – Fr 10am – 4pm, Sa 10am – 5pm.**

MADE IN JAPAN

Your favourite restaurants – Chin Chin, Attica, Circa – shop at Made in Japan. You should too. The shop stocks surprisingly affordable ceramics sourced directly from the Gifu Prefecture in Japan, renowned for more than 1000 years. Take your time and seek out the wabi-sabi ("acceptance of imperfection", to give a limited translation) – unevenly glazed vessels and dinner plates speckled with delicate cherry blossoms, and platters with a black metallic glaze. **1 – 7 Wynyard Street, South Melbourne / 9690 0001 / Mo – Su 10am – 5pm. Other locations: Mornington, Queen Victoria Market.**

CEDAR HOSPITALITY

You could kit out an entire restaurant at this longstanding kitchenware centre – and no doubt many do. Beyond affordable glasswear and cutlery, it's where chefs buy their commercial-grade vacuum sealers and Silpat non-stick silicone mats for baking, their polycarbonate blenders and triple-decker milkshake makers (yes, they exist). Don't buy a blender that's sold on television – you want one that's equal to chef-grade abuse. **223 – 231 Brunswick Road, Brunswick / 8388 6800 Mo – Fr 8.30am – 5.30pm, Sa 9am – 4pm.**

HOTEL AGENCIES

Restaurateurs have been shopping at Hotel Agencies since 1947. The enormous 3000-square-metre showroom stocks an exhaustive range of crockery, cutlery, drinkware, kitchenware, bar-service equipment and appliances. If you're in the market for inoffensive plates and saucers, shop here for Maxwell Williams. If you skew a little fancier, select some duck-egg blue stonecast plates from Churchill. Every taste and budget is catered for. **298 Nicholson Street, Fitzroy / 9411 8888 Mo – Fr 8.30am – 5.30pm, Sat 9am – 1.30pm.**

SCULLERYMADE

Scullerymade has been supplying Melbourne's chefs with the best in European kitchenware for 40 years. The product range features an aston-ishing 4000 items, many of which the shop imports directly. It's the place to come for Krüger handmade knives or elegant oven-to-table porcelain by French brand Apilco. But where it really shines is with its selection of copper cookware, much of which you'd be hard-pressed to find outside of France (or even there, for that matter). **1400 High Street Malvern / 9509 4003 Mo – Fr 9am – 5pm, Sa 9am – 1pm.**

CHEF'S ARMOURY

You don't have to spend a lot of money to get quality Japanese steel. Chef's Armoury offers blades from $130, starting with the Hachi, an all-purpose knife by modernist maker Mcusta Zanmai. It's laser-cut rather than stamped like a mass-produced knife. At the other end of the spectrum is the $2400 Konosuke "Waning Crescent Moon" single-bevelled sushi-slicing *yanagiba*, capped with buffalo horn. If you already have a Japanese knife, the staff will sharpen it to mildly terrifying levels. **422 Church Street, Richmond / 9429 1139 / Mo – Sa 10.30am – 5pm.**

RIGHT Mud.

MUD

Mud creates porcelain ceramics with a clean aesthetic and expert craftsmanship. The colour palette of velvety pinks, earthy greens and sky blues has seduced everyone from David Chang of Momofuku fame to Australian chef Bill Granger, and each piece is timeless and emotional – simple shapes with touch marks that remain. Whether it's a classic oval platter or a tall, peaked jug, every piece is distinctly sculptural and highly tactile. **181 Gertrude Street, Fitzroy / 9419 5161 / Mo – Fr 10am – 6pm, Sa 10am – 5pm, Su 12pm – 5pm.**

A BROADSHEET BOOK

A Cut Above

with STEPHANIE STAMATIS

Stephanie Stamatis chooses flowers for a living – at least, that's part of her alter ego's role as stylist Stephanie Somebody. Curating shoots for clients such as Kinfolk, Myer, Brown Brothers, Maxwell Williams and Penguin Publishing, Stamatis understands the importance of freshly cut blooms. "I think it's innate, wanting to bring the outside in, and that connection to nature," she says. "Flowers are a kind of quintessential beauty we can control within our homes."

Choosing flowers is like choosing vegetables: they're at their best when they're in season. "If it's seasonal, it will be in the best condition it can be, because it's just been picked and gone straight into the shop," Stamatis explains. "If it's not seasonal it means it's been imported or refrigerated a few months. That means once you get it into your house and it warms up a bit it's going to start disintegrating pretty quickly."

The easiest way to find out what's in season is to talk to the person who knows best. "I am constantly in conversation with florists," Stamatis says. "They want to have a conversation with you about where their flowers are coming from, so it's just about initiating that conversation." She swears by Fitzroy's Flowers Vasette. "They have one of the best ranges in a really big shop, and it's incredibly beautiful," she says. "They also have a farm, so that's why they have slightly interesting, different flowers than most."

Once you get your flowers home, make sure to cut the stems. "Trim the ends and put them in fresh water straight away," she says. "And pull off all the leaves that are going to be in the water. They're the ones that rot and make your water stink after a few days."

She also recommends focusing on one type of flower rather than arranging complicated bouquets. "If I'm having people over for dinner I just buy a single type of flower and scatter them in vases down the table," she says. "That way there's just that single element, and it looks a lot more refined. I want flowers in my house to seem effortless."

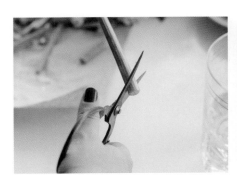

Index

Broadsheet Melbourne Food

Writer
Tim Grey

Consulting Editor
Caroline Clements

Subeditors
Louise Baxter
Miriam Kauppi
Jenny Valentish

Art Direction & Design
The Company You Keep

Illustrator
Alice Oehr

Indexer
Max McMaster

Feature Photography
Simon Shiff
Gareth Sobey
Nikki To

Photography
Jaz Blom
Thomas Brooke
Alana Dimou
Rez Harditya
Brook James
Rachel Korinek
Kristoffer Paulsen
Amy Pearson
Lindsey Rendell
Mark Roper

Simon Shiff
Gareth Sobey
Emily Weaving
Josie Withers

With thanks to
Sofya Daroy
Pitzy Folk
Pascale Gomes-McNabb
Rhys Gorgol
Penny Gow
In Bed Store
Melissa Leong-Jones
Veronica Lethorn
The Locals Market
Jamie and Loren McBride
Sophie McComas
Mat Pember
Murdoch Produce
Stefanie Reilly
Imogene Roache
Joe Rubbo
Dillon Seitchik-Reardon
Ben Siero
Stephanie Stamatis
Celine Tan
Jean Thamthanakorn and
Sarin Rojanametin

Printed & Bound
Immij

Broadsheet Media

Publisher & Director
Nick Shelton

Strategic Projects Director
Alice Wilkinson

Editorial Director
Tim Fisher

Directory Editor
Nick Connellan

A Broadsheet Book

Published in 2017 by Broadsheet
Media Pty Ltd. Level 1, 231 Smith Street,
Fitzroy, VIC 3065, Australia.

Broadsheet is a trade mark used under
licence by Broadsheet Media Pty Ltd
from BM IP Pty Ltd as trustee for the
BM IP Trust.

ISBN — 978-0-646-97848-2